GET REAL

by Mara Rockliff

GET REAL

by Mara Rockliff

RUNNING PRESS
PHILADELPHIA · LONDON

To Doug, for everything

This book is printed on 100% recycled paper using
soy-based inks.

The printer of this book is certified by the ICTI or
International Council of Toys Industry. One of ICTI's
mandates is to ensure that toys and related product
are produced in safe and humane environments.

9   8   7   6   5   4   3   2   1
Digit on the right indicates the number of this printing

Library of Congress Cataloging-in-Publication Number
2009928293

ISBN 978-0-7624-3745-0

Illustrations by Ryan Hayes
Designed by Ryan Hayes and
    Frances J. Soo Ping Chow
Typography: Archer and Verlag
Edited by T.L. Bonaddio

Running Press Book Publishers
2300 Chestnut Street
Philadelphia, PA 19103-4371

Visit us on the web!
www.runningpress.com

CONTENTS

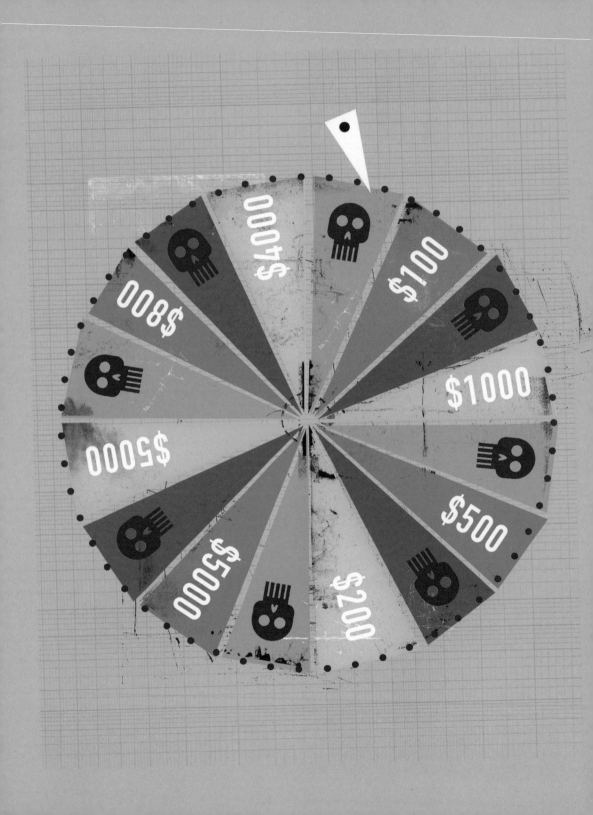

THE PRICE IS WRONG

Why it matters where your money goes.

You're going to be on TV! You're a contestant on the new show *Real Deal*.

They've slathered you with makeup, told you how to smile, and pushed you out to face the cameras. Sweat dripping down your neck, you squint into the lights and tell yourself, *Relax! It'll be fun.*

"Welcome to *Real Deal*, where what you see is what you get—and more!" the host announces. "Today, we have a special treat for you. Our young contestant here will choose between two chocolate bars. Don't they look good?" He drapes an arm around your shoulder. "Which one will you pick?"

You check out the chocolate. One bar is your favorite brand. The other bar costs more, and it's a brand you've never heard of, with a bunch of fancy blah blah blah on it about "organic" and "fair trade."

Duh. This is way too easy.

As you grab the cheaper chocolate bar, the host grins widely. "Excellent choice. But wait! Before you take a bite, let's see what else you get."

He whips aside a curtain, and a boy steps out. He's about your age, but smaller. He looks like he hasn't eaten in a week.

"This boy has never tasted chocolate in his life," the beaming host informs you. "But he works in the cocoa fields every day from dawn till dark. Sometimes he's so tired, he just falls down. Then they beat him until he gets up again."

What *is* this? All you were supposed to do was pick a candy bar . . . right?

The host goes on, "His family lives in a distant country. They're extremely poor, and they sent him away with a man who promised he would earn good wages. Actually, he doesn't get paid at all. He's a slave."

A *slave*? Wasn't that over a long time ago?

Spreading his hands, he smiles. "That's what it takes to make chocolate so cheap. Sure, the company spends millions every week on advertising. But they need to do that. Otherwise, how would they get to be your favorite brand?"

You look down at the chocolate bar, then at the boy. He stares back at you. Suddenly, you don't feel so hungry.

"Go ahead," the host urges. "Unwrap it. Eat it. Oh, but first—"

Strapping a tank on his back, he points a metal hose at you and starts spraying. Clouds of white powder rain down on you, the half-unwrapped chocolate, and the boy.

"Don't worry about him!" the host yells. "He's used to it!"

Choking, you gasp out, "What *is* that stuff?"

"Poison," he says cheerfully. "They spray it on the cocoa plants to kill the bugs. Of course, it's not so good for people, either. But don't worry. You won't taste it."

This is insane. "Okay!" you say. "I change my mind. I pick the other one!"

But the host doesn't hear you. He's already running off the stage.

A moment later, he comes roaring back—behind the wheel of a giant bulldozer. Leaning out, he hollers, "Hop in, kid! We've got a lot of rainforest to flatten!"

As he hauls you in the open window, the camera zooms in on your kicking legs, and the show's theme song booms out: *On* Real Deal . . . *you get the real deal!*

*

Okay, it's outrageous. It's ridiculous. (Though not a whole lot more outrageous than some stuff they really do show on TV.) And probably, you'd never sign up to be on a show like this.

But here's the real deal: You're on right now, like it or not. We all are.

Buy a pair of sneakers, and where does your money go? Maybe it goes to pay the guy who runs the company. He rakes in a multi-million-dollar salary—thousands of dollars every *hour*. That's a lot of sneaker sales! Of course, he doesn't actually sell—or make—the sneakers. In fact, he may never even see the Chinese factory where they are made. But his flunkeys push the factory owner to sell them sneakers at a low, low price. Then the company sells you the sneakers at a not-so-low price, and pockets a nice fat profit. Everybody's happy . . . other than the teenage girls who toil in a fume-filled sneaker factory for eighteen cents an hour.

Order a cheeseburger at the drive-up window, and what are you really buying? What's between the buns is bad enough—greasy ground-up mystery meat mixed up from hundreds of different cows, with a bunch of chemicals thrown in to give it a fake yummy taste. But your burger also comes with a super-sized side of trouble: everything from fat, unhealthy kids to poisoned rivers to global warming that is being made worse by (believe it or not) *cow farts*.

Spend your birthday money on a video game console, and you get a lot more than you bargained for. What you pull out of the package contains only about 5 percent of all the raw materials it took to make the product and get it to you. Five percent! The rest is waste. And when it breaks or a new version comes out, the console will be waste too. Toxic waste, chock-full of killer chemicals that end up in our air and water.

Is any of this your fault?

No.

Does it matter?

Yes.

Can you do anything about it?

Absolutely!

Lots of young people—and older people, too—are taking a hard look at where their money's going. Some call it "ethical consuming" or "socially conscious shopping." Some just call it "buying better." Whatever you like to call it, it's definitely on the rise. People are sick of squeezing their eyes shut like baby birds and letting companies stuff who-knows-what into their gaping gullets. Instead, they're asking questions like *Who made it?* and *What's in it?* and *What's it doing to the earth, to other people, and to me?*

Buying better just makes sense. Of course we want to buy things that don't make us sick, or ruin other people's lives, or trash the planet. And most Americans really do care about these issues. For instance, in one poll, nine out of ten teens said they would switch brands to help a cause. In another poll, at least three people out of four said they were willing to pay more for products made under good working conditions. But how many actually did? Just one in four.

What's stopping them?

What's stopping *you*?

See if any of this sounds familiar:

It's my money. Why shouldn't I buy what I want?

Go ahead! But first, check out the hidden costs of out-of-control consumerism in chapter 1, The THING That Ate the World (page 13). Then turn to chapter 2, Scammed! (page 23), for a look at how smart, savvy kids like you get tricked into buying a bunch of junk.

Come on, it can't be that bad! And even if it is, it's not *my* problem—is it?

Well . . . yes. And yes. Take a deep breath, hold your nose, and jump into reality with chapter 3, And All I Got Was This Lousy T-Shirt (page 31), chapter 4, A Peek Between the Buns (page 41), and chapter 5, Trash Talk (page 49). Warning: might make you a little queasy.

I just buy what's at the mall. What else am I supposed to do?

Glad you asked! That's what this book is really all about. You'll find plenty of outside-the-big-box choices—and their pros and cons—in chapter 6, So Long, Frankenfoods (page 57), chapter 7, Buys in the 'Hood (page 67), and chapter 8, Sweeter Treats (page 75).

Okay, I know I should buy better, but it just doesn't sound like *fun*.

Oh, yeah? Check out the cool designs in chapter 9, Makin' It (page 81)—taking green to the extreme!

All the companies *say* they're helping people and taking care of the earth. How do I know who's telling the truth?

It's not easy, but it's not impossible. Chapter 10, Green Warriors vs. Greenwashers (page 89), helps you tell the good guys from the phonies. Power to the people!

What you *won't* find in this book is a "buy better" shopping list of brand-name products you should spend your money on and companies you can support. (Though, at the end of each chapter and at the back of the book, you'll learn where to go to find out more.) Instead, you'll get the big picture: where your money's going, why it matters, and what you can do to make a difference.

Can we really change the world with our wallets? We already do.

What kind of world are *you* buying?

Let's find out.   .

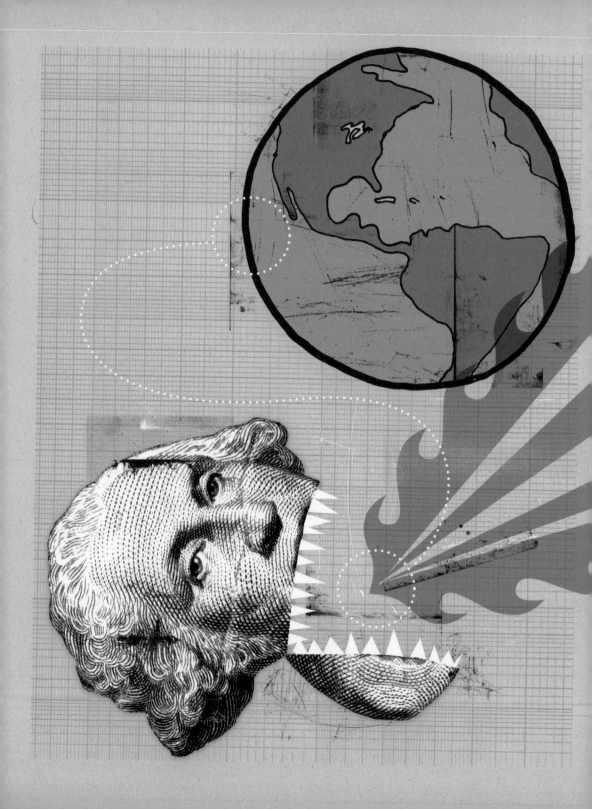

Chapter 1

THE THING THAT ATE THE WORLD

Stop it before it consumes us all!

Picture the world as a big, round, yummy-looking pie. Blueberry, maybe.

Now picture twenty kids standing around the pie. "Me first," says one pushy kid, and cuts a whopping slice. It's way bigger than one-twentieth of the pie. In fact, it's more like one-third!

The other kids crowd forward, grabbing what they can. A few get nice fat slices. Most walk away with a lot less than their fair share. Seven or eight kids are left standing at the table, staring at one single skinny slice of pie.

That pushy, greedy kid who took so much? That's us.

In the year 2000, the United States and Canada had just over 5 percent of the world's people. But their consumer spending—all the stuff families buy—added up to nearly 32 percent. Meanwhile, the purchases of all the people in South Asia, Africa, and the Middle East—more than 37 percent of the world's population—totaled less than 5 percent.

What does this mean? A lot of kids aren't getting what they need: warm clothes, enough to eat, a roof over their heads. Over a billion people live on less than one dollar a day. That's one person out of every six!

Meanwhile, some of us have so much junk we don't know what to do with it.

Houses today are twice as big as they were fifty years ago. And yet, thousands of new self-storage places spring up each year to catch the spillover of stuff Americans aren't using, have no place to put, and probably should never have bought in the first place.

Obviously, not having enough is a huge problem. But aside from a crammed closet, what could be wrong with having too much?

Here's something we all know but may not think about too often:

Everything we have comes from the earth.

Not just things like tulips and potatoes. *Everything.*

No, iPods don't grow on trees, and you can't plant a flip phone in your garden. But what they're made of does come from the earth.

Plastic, for instance, is made from oil—just like the oil we use to fuel our cars. Like potatoes, oil comes from underground. But while spuds grow in a few months, oil takes a little longer. Millions of years, in fact! The oil we are using now is older than the dinosaurs. Once it is gone, there won't be any more. And we're burning it up at the breakneck pace of eighty million barrels a day—a quarter of that in the United States alone.

How much is left? No one is sure. But it is running out.

So why are we wasting our precious oil on plastic cling wrap? On junk mail CDs? On trashy toys kids play with once or twice, then throw away?

REBELS WITH A CAUSE

You know those flimsy plastic bags they hand out at the supermarket? Americans throw out 100 billion of them a year—and they can sit in landfills for a thousand years!

Sixteen-year-old Daniel Burd was sick of plastic bags raining down on him every time he opened the closet door. So he got to work discovering bacteria that nibble plastic. With their help, he demonstrated how a plastic bag can break down in as little as three months. Daniel's project won the Canada-Wide Science Fair and netted him a $30,000 prize.

Some resources are "renewable." Rain keeps falling. Trees grow. Every spring, the birds build nests and lay their eggs to hatch new baby birds. But "renewable" does not mean "limitless." If people pump water from the ground faster than it's replaced, after a while there isn't much water left. If we chop down forests faster than they can grow back, pretty soon we run out of wood. And if we destroy the places birds and other animals live, it won't be long before the animals all disappear.

Let's go back to the pie. If one kid gobbles up more than his share, then less is left to go around. For everybody in the world to consume as much as North Americans do, we'd need five more planets just like this one.

A bulldozer pushes waste into a landfill.
Image © Serhiy Zavalnyuk / iStock

There are no more pies.

Want to know what happens when we take too much? Just watch the news. Armies fighting wars for oil. Miners ripping up tons of rock to reach an ounce of gold. Native people driven off their land so that big logging companies can gobble up the rainforest. Peaceful protesters tortured and killed.

None of this is any fun to think about. It's a huge bummer. And to make it worse, now you're supposed to give up everything you like and never shop again, right?

Wrong.

Here's the crazy thing. Some folks out there are hurting other people and wrecking the planet so that they can sell you stuff that *you don't even want*. Not really. Not if you think about it even for one minute.

Take bottled water.

Healthy. Refreshing. Convenient. How would we ever do without it?

Actually, we would do a whole lot better. Bottled water is terrible for the earth. It's bad for the people who live near the bottling plants. And it's not particularly great for all the thirsty kids plunking down their allowances on something they could get for free. But it's *fantastic* for the water bottlers, who sell it at a higher price than soda, milk, or even gasoline!

Americans drink bottled water by the billions of gallons. Making all those plastic bottles takes a million and a half barrels of oil. That's enough to gas up 100,000 cars

for a year! Then every single bottle gets on a truck, ship, or plane and travels from, say, Maine to Oregon (3,500 miles) or the island of Fiji to Florida (over 7,000 miles), burning lots more oil on the way—which adds to global warming. Altogether, so much energy is used on bottled water that one scientist compared it to filling each bottle up a quarter of the way with oil.

Must be pretty special water, huh?

Nope.

A group of scientists from the Natural Resources Defense Council spent four years testing over a hundred different brands of bottled water. Here's what they learned: Bottled water is *less* safe and pure than water we get from the tap.

How can this be?

Tap water is checked regularly to meet rules laid down by the Environmental Protection Agency. Bottled water, on the other hand, doesn't get tested very often. Put bubbles in it, and the law says it doesn't have to be tested at all! So if you open up a bottle of water, you don't know *what* you're getting. But those scientists do. When they looked at bottled water, they found lots of scary stuff, from arsenic (a poison) to "fecal coliform" (also known as poop).

The Environmental Working Group in Washington, D.C., ran its own test in 2008. In ten brands of bottled water, they found thirty-eight different chemicals, including the radioactive element strontium. ("Buy

Plastic bottles clog Bicaz lake, Romania.
Image © Stéphane Bidouze / iStock

our water! Quenches thirst *and* makes your guts glow in the dark!")

The good news is, at least a quarter of the bottled water sold in the United States is just as safe to drink as tap water. How do we know? Because it *is* tap water, drawn from public pipes and run through filters. But you'll pay up to 10,000 times more than if you filtered it at home.

POWER TO THE PEOPLE

What's "PWS"? Not too long ago, those three mysterious letters appeared on every Aquafina water bottle, along with a pretty mountain-sunset logo suggesting the water came from a clear mountain stream. But under pressure from the watchdog group Corporate Accountability International, the company agreed to spell it out: Public Water Source. In other words, Aquafina is filtered tap water.

For their cable TV show, the performers Penn & Teller took over a fancy restaurant in California. They printed menus charging up to seven bucks a bottle for imported water with elegant-sounding names like "L'eau du Robinet." Then they filmed restaurant patrons sipping water, comparing different brands, and praising their "clean" taste. What these people didn't know was that the waiter had filled all the bottles from a garden hose out back. *L'eau du Robinet* is French for "tap water."

The high price we pay for bottled water doesn't end at the cash register. Few plastic water bottles ever get recycled. The vast majority end up in landfills, where they'll take thousands of years to decompose. Or they are melted in incinerators, spewing toxic chemicals into the air. (That is, any toxic chemicals that didn't already peel off into your water.) Or they just lie around littering public parks, beaches, and sidewalks.

From a thoughtful shopper's point of view, bottled water is worse than worthless. But that same water is priceless to the people who live near the source.

HOW LOW CAN THEY GO?

Check out this Starbucks offer: Buy a bottle of Ethos Water for $1.80, and they'd give a nickel to "help children around the world get clean water." Hmm . . . How about we fill our bottles from the tap, then donate the whole $1.80 to a group like the Blue Planet Project, which fights for water justice against greedy corporations?

Ask the people of Plachimada, a village in the southwest part of India. They had all the water that they needed, until Coca-Cola set up a bottling plant and started pumping millions of liters a day. Soon wells ran dry and village girls were forced to trudge hot, dusty miles to fetch water they could cook and wash in without getting sick. After years of protests, the courts finally forced Coca-Cola to shut down its pumps. Of course, the company sent out a swarm of lawyers to appeal the case all the way up to the Indian Supreme Court. Meanwhile, the clean, fresh groundwater—a gift of nature that used to be plentiful and free—is gone.

Or ask the Fiji islanders. Fewer than half can count on having safe water to drink. Yet every day, a factory churns out a million bottles of pure FIJI Water and ships them to stores in the United States, a country where drinkable water gushes from the tap.

Or ask the folks in California, Michigan, New Hampshire, and other states who have banded together in local citizens' groups to fight Nestlé. They claim the company is draining springs, polluting rivers, killing fish—and making a mint by selling water that belongs to all of us.

No doubt about it, bottled water is a big fat rip-off. But it's also just one example. Everything we buy has hidden costs.

Who takes out the garbage in your house? If it's your job, you may not be surprised to hear that every one of us throws out, on average, 4.6 pounds of trash a day. Multiply that by over 300,000,000 Americans, and you're seriously talking trash.

In a single day, McDonald's serves up enough garbage to fill the Empire State Building. And that's just what the customers leave behind. How much is getting tossed out back? Ask Ronald.

But the garbage in our cans is just a tiny portion of the waste we actually create. As Annie Leonard points out in her online video, *The Story of Stuff*, "For every one garbage can of waste you put out on the curb, seventy garbage cans of waste were made upstream." (*Upstream* means everything that happens from the time the raw materials are taken from the earth until the item ends up in your hands.)

Take a look around your room. Pick up something you bought yourself. Now picture a pile of garbage seventy times its size.

If that garbage was displayed beside the item at the store, would you still buy it?

Of course, that will never happen. The people who churn out this stuff don't want you to think about what it really costs. They want you to buy more, more, more.

But isn't that what you're supposed to do? Shouldn't you be a good consumer?

Drag out your old dictionary and look up the word *consume*. It means "destroy, devour, squander, swallow up." Yuck. Not exactly what you want to see when you look in the mirror.

Sure, consuming is a part of life. We all do it. We enjoy it. We don't want to stop.

The same goes for sleeping—and we spend more hours sleeping than eating or shopping. But when was the last time you heard anyone mention "the American sleeper"?

Getting Americans to think of themselves mainly as consumers—not as friends, neighbors, family members, citizens, students, athletes, artists, dancers, or nose pickers—is a giant, nasty hoax. Maybe corporations think we were all put on earth to buy their stuff. But we were not.

ACT OUT!

On Thanksgiving Day, Americans sit down together at their tables and give thanks for what they have. Then the next day, they rush out and grab more. Sometimes the bargain-hunting frenzy spins out of control—as in 2008, when overeager shoppers stormed a Wal-Mart on Long Island, smashing the glass doors and trampling a store employee. Looking for a saner way to spend the day after Thanksgiving? Celebrate Buy Nothing Day instead. Do anything that's free and fun . . . and stay out of the stores!

Some people will tell you it's your patriotic duty to buy as much as possible. Consumer spending makes the economy grow. The more it grows, the happier and richer we all are.

You already know one big problem with this argument. We only have one planet, and it isn't growing. So we can't go on using up more and more of it forever.

But there's another problem. When people talk about how the economy is doing, they are looking at the value of all the goods and services produced in the United States. They add it all up into a number called the "gross domestic product" (GDP), then divide it by the country's population.

The GDP would be a pretty good way of figuring out how much each of us has—if everybody got an equal share in real life. But as any second grader knows, we don't. Some Americans are Richie Rich, and some are Little Orphan Annie. So a sky-high GDP won't necessarily earn you, your family, or anyone you know a single penny.

Also—please don't gag—but money can't buy happiness. It's a scientific fact! Studies show that once people have enough money for the things they really need, like food and clothes and a roof over their heads, getting even more money doesn't make them any happier.

Politicians, CEOs, and news anchors are very hung up on the GDP. (Maybe all that hairspray clouds their brains.) But it's not the only way to measure how we're doing. Way back in 1972, the king of Bhutan came up with the GNH: gross national happiness. While the GDP looks at one thing—consuming—the GNH examines four: fairness, environmental conservation, culture, and good government.

Cool, huh?

Another measure is the GPI, or genuine

progress indicator, created by the think tank Redefining Progress. Unlike the GNH, it uses money as its basis, so it can be backed up with hard numbers. But unlike the GDP, those numbers take account of inequality, crime, pollution, loss of free time, and other hidden costs. So while the GDP goes up, up, up, the GPI hasn't been going anywhere.

Okay. Enough with all the Gs. Why so much talk about consuming being bad? Isn't this supposed to be a book about how to buy better?

Sure. And now you're ready to take the first step—asking the right questions. Such as:

Do I need this? Do I want it? Will it make me happy?

What went into making this? Who was hurt—or helped?

How much stuff did this use up? How much garbage will it leave behind?

There are lots more questions you can ask, and you'll discover them as we go on. But now, let's talk about some people who don't want you asking questions. People who will gladly twist the truth, make you feel like a loser, and spend billions of dollars to keep you from asking yourself anything at all before you buy.

They're known as advertisers.

MORE

- Ready for twenty minutes of gloves-off, in-your-face truth—with cartoons? Click on *The Story of Stuff* (storyofstuff.com) to find out where all that stuff in the stores comes from and where it goes after we toss it out.
- What's so scary about bottled water? Find out more—and join the fight—at Think Outside the Bottle (thinkoutsidethebottle.org).
- Billed as "the movie Santa doesn't want you to see," *What Would Jesus Buy?* follows the Reverend Billy and the Church of Stop Shopping Gospel Choir on a road trip across America to rescue Christmas from the Shopocalypse.

Chapter 2

SCAMMED!

Think you're hip to advertising?
Think again . . .

Okay. Pop quiz. How many times a day do you get hit by advertising messages?

(a) 50

(b) 100

(c) 500

(d) Who cares? Other kids might fall for ads, but they don't affect *me*.

If you answered (a), (b), or (c), you're not even close. The average American kid sees and hears 3,000 advertising messages a day. Take out the eight hours you're asleep, and that's more than three a minute!

We're not just talking TV commercials here. In fact, TV is probably the least of it. After all, skipping commercials is pretty simple. (Though most kids still watch 40,000 of them every year.) But what about the slogan on your T-shirt and the logo on your butt? The jingles you hear piped in at the mall? The texted ads that clog your cell phone, and the flashing ads that catch your eye each time you get online?

What about the sports arena named after a soda? Or the concert "brought to you" by a big sneaker brand? What about the new blockbuster movie you see everywhere, from the paper bag your burger comes in to the tie-in video game?

Back when your parents were kids, companies spent about $100 million a year advertising to children and teenagers. Today, they spend that much every couple of *days*. The steady trickle of ads has turned into a raging, roaring flood.

Maybe you're not worried about getting swept away. You grew up with this stuff. Sure, some kids might buy a jacket just because they saw an actor wear one like it on their favorite TV show. But you buy what you like.

Guess what? That's exactly what those kids are thinking about you.

In one study, 462 seventh and eighth graders were asked what they thought about "product placement" (slipping brand names into movies, books, TV shows, and video games). Some of the students said product placement was okay. Some said it wasn't. But *every single one* of them believed their friends would be more easily influenced by this advertising than they would them-selves. And kids they didn't know? Ha! Those chumps would fall for anything.

Reality check time. Remember all those millions of dollars going into advertising aimed at kids? It adds up to $16.8 billion a year. No one spends that kind of money unless they're getting results. Sure, young people today are more sophisticated than ever before. But so are advertisers.

HOW LOW CAN THEY GO?

To promote its caffeinated candy bar, Butterfinger invited customers to shave their heads and stencil "Butterfinger Buzz" in orange paint where their hair used to be—then upload photos to the company Web site. The payoff? A coupon for *one* free Butterfinger bar.

Let's talk about who the people behind advertising really are. They're not the gor-geous, trendy, twinkly-toothed young actors you see in commercials. They're not movie stars or athletes or any other kind of celebrity. And they're definitely not adorable cartoons or pumped-up video game avatars.

Here's a little secret: Advertisers are not even cool.

Check it out yourself. Each year, they hold a conference called "Kid Power," where they give awards to advertisers who did the best job at getting kids to buy stuff. ("Kid power" to them means having power *over* kids.) Feel like a little cyber sleuthing? See if you can Google photos of the latest winners.

Yes. It's true. These people look just like . . . parents and teachers.

Only, advertisers are not thinking about how to get you to eat broccoli or read poetry or do anything else they believe is good for you. They don't even care what's good for you. When they look at kids, there's nothing in their eyes but big fat dol-lar signs.

Want to know what they *are* thinking about? Take a look at what they read:

The Great Tween Buying Machine: Cap-turing Your Share of the Multi-Billion-Dollar Tween Market.

The $100 Billion Allowance: How to Get Your Share of the Global Teen Market.

Creating Ever-Cool.

Kidfluence.

*BRAND*Child.

Books like these all seem to start out the same way, rubbing their hands and gloating about all the money that kids spend. Then they teach advertisers how to use your deepest fantasies and darkest fears to get you to spend all that money on stuff you don't really want or need.

REBELS WITH A CAUSE

When a group of teenage girls in Pennsylvania saw the Abercrombie & Fitch ads, they were totally grossed out. T-shirts with WHO NEEDS BRAINS WHEN YOU HAVE THESE printed across the chest? No way! So they launched a "girlcott" of the company.

One *Today Show* spot and hundreds of news stories later, Abercrombie & Fitch pulled the shirts. But the girlcotters didn't stop there. They started their own T-shirt line, with slogans like BEAUTY COMES FROM WITHIN, AND I'M GORGEOUS and YOUR FUTURE BOSS.

Make you feel unpopular? Ugly? Uncool? Convince you that your life will change if you just buy their latest product . . . and the next one . . . and then the one after that . . .? Hey, it's all in a day's work.

And how do they feel about it? Just fine, thanks. As a CEO of MTV once bragged, when asked about his channel's influence on teenagers: "We don't just influence them—we *own* them."

Of course, the advertising biz isn't all cotton candy. They have to work hard, finding new ways to keep kids (or, as they like to call you, "developing consumers") from wising up and thinking for themselves.

Here's one way they do it: advertise to babies. No, babies don't have any money. But they grow up into kids with money. And when they do, advertisers want them to have a nice warm fuzzy feeling about that One Special Brand—a feeling that goes so far back they can't remember how it started.

Do you feel a tiny familiar thrill when you see the golden arches of McDonald's? Or the Disney castle, all aglow with sparkling fairy dust? How about the Coca-Cola logo, or the Nike swoosh? Maybe it's because you've known them all your life. By age three, the typical American child has learned to recognize 100 brand logos— and *love* them. That's what advertisers call "cradle to grave loyalty." They also call it "owning" kids.

But brainwashing babies is just the beginning. After all, there are a lot of brands out there—at least 900,000 at last count. How can they make sure you don't forget theirs?

One answer is LOTS AND LOTS OF ADS. Ads everywhere. Ads all the time. Giant ads spray-painted on the sides of buildings. Tiny ads lasered onto eggs. Ads at the beach, stamped in the sand, or painted on the sides of cows out grazing in a field. Ads plastered all over park benches, in a public bathroom, on the sides of buses that drive by. Ads tattooed on human bodies. One advertiser even tried to launch a "space billboard" so big and bright it could outshine the moon!

POWER TO THE PEOPLE

Twelve thousand billboards went blank in São Paulo, Brazil, in 2007, thanks to a "Clean City Law." The ban on outdoor ads even included the sky, as advertisers found out when they tried to fly over the city in a plane plastered with cartoon pictures from *The Simpsons*. As Homer Simpson would say: "D'oh!"

Then there is "synergy." That's corporate talk for "let's advertise each other." Synergy is why it's sometimes hard to tell two companies apart. Remember McDisney? Until a few years ago, if you went into a McDonald's, the latest Disney movie would hit you from every direction. And if you went to the Magic Kingdom, you'd be unlikely to get out again without sampling Mickey D's.

More and more, though, what you're dealing with is really one huge company. Let's say Warner Brothers brings out a new movie. It's a great big splash. You see it on HBO, CNN, the WB, and the Cartoon Network. You read about it in *Time, Entertainment Weekly,* and *People.* Must be a terrific flick— or maybe it's just that Time Warner owns all these media outlets, and dozens more.

Still, you can always turn off the computer, click the red button on the TV remote, and stay out of the magazine aisle. Advertisers hate that. They don't want kids to have a choice of whether to look at their ad or not. Why would they? So they go where they can find a captive audience— your school.

Any of these ring a (school) bell?
- brand-name vending machines in the cafeteria
- ads on book covers, on screen savers, in classrooms and in hallways, on the scoreboard in the gym, on the school Web site, even on the roof
- commercials playing on the school bus radio

- students told they can't sell juice or hot cocoa at a bake sale because their school has signed a contract with a soda bottler
- teachers forbidden to fast-forward through commercials on Channel One news shows
- principals pushing kids to buy more junk food from school sponsors
- classes taken on field trips to auto dealerships and chain stores
- free "educational" materials with slanted facts (like lessons from a logging company suggesting they clear-cut forests to help wildlife)
- kids assigned to come up with an ad campaign or design a new product, which their teacher then turns over to the company
- fast food coupons as rewards for good report cards

Why would schools sell out their students? Ask your principal or school board, and they'll say it's all about the Benjamins. Schools just don't have the funds they need. But way back when your principal was a pimply teen, schools were pretty much ad-free, and they got along fine. So where did all the money go?

Three little words: corporate tax cuts.

In the old days, companies paid taxes, and some of that money went to schools. But for years now, they've been paying less. Much less. So the big companies are rich, and schools are poor. Put it another way: all that money those nice companies hand out, just for the chance to advertise to you at school? That was *your* money.

It's the same with all the other corporate-sponsored public places and events. Why are stadiums, theaters, libraries, and hospitals named after multinational companies, rather than local heroes? Why are city buses plastered with eye-popping advertisements? Why is every festival and concert hung with giant banners from the companies that "made it possible"?

When public money was still public, the people decided together how to spend it. Now the corporations get to choose—and what they've chosen is to slam us with 3,000 advertising messages a day.

ACT OUT!

Sick of ads yammering at you all day long? Why not talk back? Find an ad you hate and "adbust" it to say what you think it should say. Then hang it on your locker door, post it online, or enter it in the yearly Counter Ad Contest run by the New Mexico Media Literacy Project.

Bad news for us, but great news for the advertisers.

Or is it? Maybe people get fed up. Maybe they just stop listening. As an advertising bigwig once complained, "Consumers are like roaches—you spray them and spray them, and they get immune after a while."

So the advertisers shrug and just give up, right?

Yeah, right.

In the world of advertising, when the going gets tough, the tough get tricky. Manipulative. Downright deceptive.

You already know about product placement. It's big on TV, especially reality TV. Those people don't just happen to be texting on cell phones from that one company. And they're not eating that brand of fast-food sandwiches because they like them. It's all planned—and often paid for to the tune of millions. It's worth the money, because viewers can't skip the commercials. The show *is* commercials.

NO WAY!

In just three months, the Nielsen Company counted 3,291 product placements on the TV show *American Idol*. That's more than 131 per episode! Wonder how they squeezed in time for actual commercial breaks. . . .

Product placement in video games is even better. A TV show, you'll probably watch once. A movie, maybe a few times. But video games, you play over and over and over. And you're not just watching. You are in the game. For the time that you are playing it, you *are* that rock star guzzling Red Bull or that skateboarder tuning in to SIRIUS Satellite Radio.

But maybe you're hip to all this. Maybe you totally despise commercial culture. You go for what's different, funky, independent, *real*.

They're after you, too.

Think advertising is a joke? They'll feed you an ironic "anti-ad" ad campaign—and laugh all the way to the bank.

Into the indie scene? It's fresh. It's new. It hits their radar. Next thing you know, you see your fresh new style in Old Navy or on MTV.

Care about causes, not labels? Advertisers scurry off for a crash course on How to Market with a Heart. (Of course, some companies really are doing right and need to get the word out. We'll talk about that in chapter 10, Green Warriors vs. Greenwashers.)

Okay, so you can't trust advertisers. Thank you, Captain Obvious. So what? When you want to know what's cool, you go to other kids. School friends. Sports friends. Online friends. Friend friends.

So do they.

You've heard about the coolhunters. They're twenty-five, thirty, forty years old, and they spend their lives running after teenagers. They talk like kids, dress like kids, and act like kids to win their trust. They pick out kids they think are cool, then pay to follow them home and dig through their closets.

Letting some thirtysomething bald guy scrounge around in your dust bunnies isn't everyone's idea of cool. Still, it's honest money compared to what the "street teams" do. Advertisers like to call it "peer to peer brand endorsement," "viral marketing," or "buzz." In plain English, it's known as faking out your friends.

These kids wander around saying things like, "Have you tried new product Z?" and "Z is really great." Or maybe they just wear Z to school (or eat it, use it, listen to it) and wait for somebody to ask. They mention Z in chat rooms, IM their friends about Z. They rave about Z in their blogs.

What they don't say is that they've been hired by the company that makes Z. Sometimes they get paid. Sometimes they get free stuff. Sometimes they just like feeling that they're part of something big.

They are. They're cogs in the machine.

If you think that sounds like some old science fiction movie like *The Matrix*, that's because it is. You walk down the street, and an "audio spotlight" beams a message straight into your head. You get online, and spies track every click to aim just the right ads at you. You glance at a commercial, and the advertisers *know* how you'll react, because they've tested it by scanning people's brains.

Remember that quiz at the beginning of the chapter, with only wrong answers? What was up with that? Just this: If you let other people tell you what your choices are, you'll never get it right.

Advertisers like to make you think you're in control. They like to offer choices. But when all those choices stink deep down, freedom is a fraud.

MORE

- *The Merchants of Cool* asks: Do media giants like MTV copy youth culture, or create it? Who is selling what to whom? Watch this PBS special on DVD or online at pbs.org.

- Know your enemy! Read *Made You Look: How Advertising Works and Why You Should Know* by Shari Graydon and Warren Clark.

- *Paka paka* cameras? Fake shampoo? Coolhunters and culture jammers go head to head in Scott Westerfeld's novel *So Yesterday.*

- If you think ads are everywhere now—what if they got hardwired into your brain? M. T. Anderson's cyberpunk novel *Feed* is a chilling vision of a future that may not be far away.

MADE
IN
CHINA
FOR
PENNIES

$19.99

Chapter 3

AND ALL I GOT WAS THIS LOUSY T-SHIRT

What they never tell you at the mall.

S o there you are, inside the store, staring at racks and racks of clothes.

Let's say you're shopping for a pair of jeans. Do you want low-rise or high-rise? Classic fit, boot-cut, wide leg, or relaxed? The deep blue kind that scream "brand new"? Or the pre-faded kind that look like you've been wearing them for years?

You may not love every single choice, like spending your last penny on the latest style versus going for the clearance item Grandma wouldn't even wear to mow the grass. But one thing is for sure—you have plenty of choices.

Or do you?

Try asking for the jeans sewn by a worker earning more than a few cents an hour. Look for the label that assures you that the denim factory didn't dump poisonous runoff into rivers. See if a sales clerk can point out the sign that says how many toxic chemicals were sprayed on the "natural cotton" that will soon be nestled close against your skin.

Of course, you don't find any of this in the store. All you see is size, price, style. So you take a pair of jeans into the dressing room and try them on. Hmm. Nice fit . . . popular brand . . . and they're on sale.

Hey, what's this scrap of paper in the pocket?

My name is Mei. I work in a factory in China. I'm fourteen years old.

The factory is many, many miles from my home. I've never been away from my family before. But they are counting on me to help out.

I live here at the factory, in a teeny room I share with twelve other girls. It's crowded, but we don't spend much time there, anyway. We're always working.

Early in the morning, when it's still dark, we go down to the factory floor. My job is to brush off lint and snip the loose threads off the jeans. We work fast, our heads down. If they catch us talking, laughing, or even looking at each other, they take it out of our pay.

They charge us for everything. The food, which tastes bad and gives me a stomachache. The hard wooden bunk beds where we sleep. The hot water that we have to haul upstairs in pails so we can wash.

At 2 am, we're still hard at work. Most nights, I sleep about four hours. But when there's a rush order, we work all night long. Sometimes they keep our eyes open with plastic clothespins.

My life wasn't always like this. I used to be a normal girl. I went to school. I helped around the house. I hung out with my friends.

I want to go home, but I can't.

My pay?
About six cents an hour.
P.S. I hope you like the jeans.

Mei's letter is made up, but the details of her life are all too real, as you can see in the film *China Blue*. Chinese factories are full of teenage girls like Mei, who come to the big city hoping for a chance to get ahead. Instead, they find themselves slaving for weeks or months with no days off and, frequently, no pay at all—the boss holds their first paycheck as a "deposit" to keep them from quitting and going home.

To avoid getting fined for falling asleep, Jasmine (17) and Li Ping (14) use clothespins that keep their eyes open.
Image © Teddy Bear Films, photo by Micha X. Peled

Or maybe it's not a pair of jeans from China. Maybe it's a pair of underpants from Bangladesh. When an American human rights group called the National Labor Committee checked out a Bangladeshi factory that was making Hanes underwear, the investigators turned up workers as young as eleven.

These kids' lives sounded a lot like Mei's. They worked at least twelve to fourteen hours every day, and often more. Some-times they worked as much as twenty hours in a single day. They might get one day off a month. And they had to work fast. One boy's job was to sew the crotch shut on each pair of underwear. For sewing 120 pairs an hour, he got fifteen cents. If he made a mistake, slowed down, or fell asleep, the boss screamed at him and sometimes hit.

The law in Bangladesh says if you are between fourteen and seventeen, you can work up to thirty hours a week, but not after 7 PM. So every night, at seven sharp, the teenage workers punched out their time cards. Then they worked on till 4 AM, unpaid.

The law also says that if you are under fourteen, you shouldn't be working at all. So when anybody came to see the factory, the younger kids had to run and hide . . . in the bathroom. Think the bathrooms at your school are skanky? Theirs had no soap, no toilet paper, and often no running water. Let's just say that after hiding in there for an hour or two, you'd be happy to get back to sewing underpants.

REBELS WITH A CAUSE

Kids slaving in factories in Vietnam or Honduras to make school T-shirts and team uniforms for kids in the United States? Appalled by the idea, students lobbied to make Brattleboro Union High School in Vermont the first U.S. high school to join the anti-sweatshop Worker Rights Consortium. But they didn't stop there. They took their cause all the

way to the statehouse. **Thanks to their hard work, in 2008 Vermont became the seventh state to make its clothing purchases officially sweat-free.**

Check your closet. Chances are, some of your clothes were made in Bangladesh or China. China makes more clothes than any other country in the world, but even tiny Bangladesh makes one billion pieces of clothing each year just for the United States. That's like a pair of pants, a T-shirt, and a sock or two for every single person in the nation!

But sweatshops—factories with long hours, low pay, and horrible conditions—aren't just in poor countries far away. They're everywhere, even in the United States and Canada. Believe it! There are fifty thousand sweatshop workers just in New York City. And the U.S. Department of Labor reports that most garment shops in Los Angeles pay workers less than the legal minimum wage.

Now, the people who run sweatshops may not be the nicest folks you'll ever meet. And you can bet the bathrooms *they* use have plenty of toilet paper.

But behind their Grinchlike attitude is something more than meanness.

It's called math.

Break it down. According to the labor rights group Sweatshop Watch, if you buy a piece of clothing for $100, the manufacturer gets about $15. If that doesn't sound too bad, ask yourself: When's the last time you paid $100 for a pair of underpants?

Well, how much *do* you pay? And what's 15 percent of that?

The world's biggest sport today isn't soccer or skateboarding or even Ping Pong. It's an extreme sport known as the "race to the bottom."

This is how it's played. A guy in a nice suit flies in from Big Brand X. . . .

Mr. X: Here's an order for a bunch of clothes. Here's when we want them: Right away. Here's what we'll pay for them: Even less than before.

Owner: But—but—it's not enough! I can't do it!

Mr. X: (*Shrugs, picks up briefcase*) No problemo. I'll go down the street and find someone who can.

Owner: (*Thinks fast*) Well . . . I could lower pay a little more . . . and keep the workers up an hour or two later. . . .

Mr. X: Now we're talking.

The race to the bottom has one simple rule: Give in or get out. If the owner won't (or can't) give a big brand the super-cheap price it demands, the order goes to someone else. And if workers refuse to toil longer hours for less pay, the owner kicks them out and hires new workers willing to take whatever they can get.

Even governments have to pull on their running shoes or pay the price. Suppose they pass a law saying that workers must be paid enough to live on, or that polluters must clean up after themselves. Or maybe they just try to enforce laws they already

CLEAN CLOTHES?

WHAT TO ASK?

Were these clothes made in a sweatshop? Hey, it's a start! And seriously, if the people in the store or at the company's main office can't give you an answer, that's an answer in itself. You have a right to know where your clothes are made, how the workers are treated, and whether they are paid enough to feed their families and send their kids to school.

How do you know? Lots of companies have codes of conduct for their suppliers. But if they really mean it, they let *independent inspectors* in who show up *unannounced* and talk to workers *off-site*, where the boss can't see or hear.

Will you come clean? Some companies hide dirty secrets behind talk of "competition" and "proprietary information." Ask if they have a list of all the factories around the world where their products are made. Does it describe the wages and working conditions at each factory? Can you see it?

WHERE TO GO?

To find out who's been naughty and who's been nice

- BehindTheLabel.org
- Clean Clothes Campaign (cleanclothes.org/companies)
- Green America National Green Pages (greenpages.org)

- Green America Responsible Shopper (responsibleshopper.org)
- SweatFree Communities Shop with a Conscience Consumer Guide (sweatfree.org/shoppingguide)

have. What happens next? The giant corporations shrug, pick up their briefcases, and head off to some other country where they'll get a cheaper deal—leaving behind empty factories, jobless workers, and, typically, a big environmental mess.

Big Brand X may whine and whimper that it's just one more runner in the race. If it doesn't get those low, low prices and a free pass to pollute, it "can't compete."

But the numbers tell another story:
- $30.6 million—what the *Wall Street Journal* reports Disney paid its CEO in 2008
- $30 million—what Avon reportedly paid actress Reese Witherspoon to be its first "global ambassador" (aka the world's richest Avon lady)
- $105 million—what Nike reportedly paid golfer Tiger Woods to wear the swoosh

The teenage workers in that factory in Bangladesh talked about their dream job. They fantasized about working only twelve hours a day, six days a week, for the huge sum of thirty-six cents an hour.

Some of the clothes they made were sold by Wal-Mart, the biggest company in the world. Wal-Mart took in $378 *billion* in 2008. This one chain has a larger economy than Austria, Denmark, Egypt, Greece, Ireland, Kenya, Lithuania, New Zealand, the Philippines, or even oil-rich Saudi Arabia—and way larger than Bangladesh.

How much would it hurt a company like that to pay a few cents more for underwear?

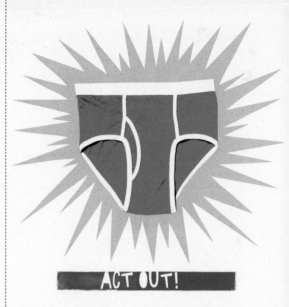

ACT OUT!

If you're not happy with what you hear about a company, don't buy their stuff—and tell them why. You can phone or e-mail, but handwritten paper letters get the most attention. Do they care what one kid thinks? Maybe not. But for each person who takes the time to write, companies figure that a bunch of other customers feel the same way. So every letter counts!

But that underwear was dirty (sorry!) long before it reached the Wal-Mart shelf. Same for that pair of jeans, that T-shirt—pretty much anything made of cotton.

Does eleven sound a little young for working in a factory? Well, guess what age some kids start working in the cotton fields? Hint: if they lived next door to you, they'd be in kindergarten.

Here's what they do instead of story time and Duck, Duck, Goose:
- In Egypt, one million kids work pulling worm eggs off the cotton plants and

squishing them between their finger and their thumb.

- In India, they're woken up at 4 AM to work. If the boss is in a bad mood that day, he beats them with a pipe.
- In Tajikistan, they get sent off to summer "holiday camps" where they pick cotton dawn to dusk, unpaid.

Why are children working in the cotton fields? Because they work for cheap (or free). And why do cotton farmers all over the world need cheap labor? Because they don't get paid much for their cotton. And why are cotton prices so low? Here's one major reason: because the United States grows lots of cotton, and it sells it all over the world, cheap.

Wait a minute. Doesn't cheap stuff come from *other* places? How can American growers sell their cotton cheaper than some African farmer who plows with a skinny ox and lives on less—maybe much less—than one dollar a day?

Welcome to the wonderful world of U.S. cotton subsidies.

"Subsidy" means "free money from the government." The U.S. government tosses out heaps and heaps of it to cotton farmers every year. Most of the money goes to the top few growers—big boys who have raked in millions of bucks apiece in subsidies. With a sweet deal like that, it isn't hard to undercut competitors on price.

According to one study, in a single year, African farmers in twenty-four countries lost a total of $302 million, thanks to U.S. cotton subsidies. That's $302 million that they would have earned selling their cotton for a fair price, if giant growers in America hadn't been paid billions in tax dollars to sell theirs cheap.

In 2007, the World Trade Organization ruled that U.S. cotton payments were illegal and unfair. But the cotton lobby still managed to cram a bale of subsidies into the U.S. Food, Conservation, and Energy Act of 2008, also known as the farm bill.

Of course, most of that money ends up in the hands of the richest growers. Meanwhile, ordinary cotton farmers are just scraping by.

Cotton is really hard to grow. If plants were people, cotton would be the delicate, sickly Southern belle. The weather's always too hot or too cold, too wet or too dry. Cotton faints dead away in a high wind. It's too weak to fight off weeds. And it's apt to be eaten alive by dozens of different kinds of pests.

With all these enemies lined up against them, farmers take any help they can get.

Cotton plants are doused with more insecticide (bug poison) than any crop in the world. Plenty of herbicide (weed poison) gets slopped on, too. In fact, it takes three-quarters of a pound of chemicals to grow the cotton for a single pair of jeans.

The problem with all this poison is— it's poison.

In Uzbekistan, kids working in the field after the pesticide is sprayed sometimes get "chicken eye." First, everything before their eyes turns white. Then they go blind. After a while, luckily, the blindness goes away. But other pesticide effects do not.

In Africa, a father left his pesticide-drenched clothes up on the roof to keep them out of reach of his four children. That night, it rained. The rain soaked through his clothes and dripped down into the family's water jugs, which they drank from the next morning. Within hours, all four children died.

In India, the kids who squirt the poison on the fields aren't given masks or gloves. (Come on—they don't even have shoes!) They mix up the concentrated chemicals with their bare hands.

But you don't have to travel all the way to Africa or India for killer chemicals. Out of the nine pesticides commonly sprayed on U.S. cotton, five are known to cause cancer. (The other four haven't been proven *not* to.) At least one of them is so deadly you could die if a single drop landed on your skin.

If spraying toxic chemicals on cotton while it's growing weren't enough, turning the cotton into cloth adds more. Harsh chlorine bleach. Formaldehyde. Caustic soda. (*Caustic* means "eats holes in things"—like skin.) Poisonous heavy metal dyes.

FAST FORWARD

Cotton may be king, but face it—royalty went out of fashion a long time ago. The weave of the future? Maybe Eco-fi, a cloth made from recycled plastic soda bottles. Or Lyocell, an eco-friendly fabric made of wood pulp. Or you may find yourself sporting seaweed, corn, soy, hemp, or bamboo.

Although scientists have tested cotton clothing and found hazardous chemicals, the cotton industry insists that practically all the nastiness is rinsed away before the clothes get to the store. So that's a relief.

Wait a minute . . . rinsed away *where*?

Hmm. Could this have anything to do with the contaminated water found in cotton-growing areas in Arkansas, Kentucky, Louisiana, Mississippi, Missouri, and Tennessee?

The outdoor gear store Patagonia switched to 100 percent organic cotton back in 1996. Asked why people often seem a lot less interested in organic clothing than organic food, Patagonia's environmental director hazarded a guess: "You don't stuff your shirt into your mouth."

Guess what, though? You sort of do.

Less than a quarter of what cotton farmers scoop up from their fields is cotton—the part of the plant that's made into the cloth. The rest, including seeds, used to be known as cotton trash. But now the farmers sell the seeds for oil. You'll find cottonseed oil in all kinds of foods: Cookies. Potato chips. Spaghetti sauce. Candy bars. Peanut butter. Salad dressing. Even breath mints.

After they squeeze the oil from the seeds, they feed what's left to farm animals. So if you drink a glass of milk or eat a plate of eggs and bacon, you may be swallowing a bit of whatever was in the cotton field—chemical pesticides, herbicides, and defoliants, or the latest craze, genetically modified organisms (also known as GMOs, or Frankenfoods).

But, hey, look on the bright side.

You probably won't feel so bad about the cotton chemicals when you find out what else is in your food.

MORE

- They giggle, they like boys, they love to dance—but they're so tired after sixteen-hour workdays that they fall asleep on the factory floor. Once you meet Jasmine and her friends in the film *China Blue*, a pair of jeans will never look the same.

- How *do* they sell those socks so cheap? *Wal-Mart: The High Cost of Low Price* peeks behind the scenes at what's been called "the world's largest, richest, and probably meanest corporation." Available on DVD.

- Find out how you can help your school, religious group, or town become sweat-free: United Students Against Sweatshops (studentsagainstsweatshops.org).

Chapter 4

A PEEK BETWEEN THE BUNS

Fast food—more disgusting than you ever dreamed.

Ever fix dinner for your family? Here's an easy recipe that everyone will love. You'll need a few simple ingredients sure to be found on any kitchen shelf:

Modified starch, autolyzed yeast extract, dextrose, sodium acid pyrophosphate, mono- and diglycerides, sodium aluminum phosphate, monocalcium phosphate, tertiary butylhydroquinone, dimethylpolysiloxane—

What? You don't have any of that?

Then how do you expect to make Chicken McNuggets?

Don't blame your parents for not keeping dimethylpolysiloxane on the spice rack.

When a chemical has been accused of making cells go mutant and grow tumors, people tend to think twice before sprinkling it on their food.

Another thing you may not find at home is tertiary butylhydroquinone, or TBHQ. According to food writer Michael Pollan, swallowing a gram of it (maybe a quarter teaspoon) would leave you sicker than a dog. But small amounts are sprayed on your fast food to keep it "fresh."

Mmmm, good.

Of course, those yummy nuggets aren't just made of icky chemicals. The good news is, they're made of chicken, too.

Wait. Maybe that's the bad news.

Where does chicken come from? If you

said "the farm," give yourself ten points. But what kind of farm? If you're picturing a nice old-timey scene, with a few chickens pecking in a barnyard while a farmer in a straw hat milks the cow, then take away—oh, let's say thirty thousand points. That's about how many chickens you'll find packed together in a giant chicken shed on a factory farm.

Factory farming is exactly what it sounds like: running a farm like a factory. Nearly all the meat in the United States now comes from factory farms. They're big. They're fast. And they treat living animals like chunks of steel or plastic rolling past on an assembly line.

Chickens on a factory farm can live their whole lives without ever seeing the sun. They're kept in sheds so crowded, it's impossible to clean them while the chickens are inside. (And if you've ever cleaned a birdcage, you know what those thirty thousand birds are sitting in.)

Each chicken's space is not much wider than this book. Crammed in like that, they tend to get stressed out and peck each other. Some farmers solve the problem by "debeaking" them, which hurts—a lot—and makes it hard for them to eat.

In a factory, the faster you can churn a product out, the more money you make. On a factory farm, that means getting chickens big enough to sell, as soon as possible. The lights are left on day and night, to keep the chickens eating instead of falling asleep. They're fed whatever's cheap and fattening, from stale pretzels to slaughterhouse scraps. (In a bizarre cannibalistic twist, these scraps are often bits of other chickens.) Many farmers even feed their chickens arsenic, a poison, to kill bugs and help the chickens grow. A chicken raised this way doesn't taste very good. That's why one of the many additives in a Chicken McNugget is—believe it or not—"chicken flavor." Yes, folks: they're trying to make chicken taste like chicken.

At this point, you might be thinking about ordering a cheeseburger instead.

Well . . . go ahead. As long as you're okay with eating pesticides, antibiotics, hormones, viruses, bacteria, chemical additives, and the results of weird experiments that range from cloning animals to shooting chunks of DNA from one species into another. Oh, yeah—and you may be chowing down on cow poop, too.

But that's not all. When you plunk down your cash for beef from a factory farm, you're also paying to:

- pollute our air and water
- kill off plants and animals
- breed scary new super-diseases
- add to global warming
- burn up a huge amount of fossil fuel*

You want fries with that?

Let's take a little field trip to a cattle feed-lot. All right, everybody off the bus—

What do you mean, you want to get back on? Yeah, sure it smells bad. Okay, it *stinks*. What did you expect? You're looking at a hundred thousand cows. Each cow lets out as much as 120 pounds of manure a day.

That's *twelve million pounds of poop*. On this one feedlot. And that's just today. There's also yesterday, the day before, and the day before that. . . .

Where does it all go? The cows are lying in it. They stomp in it, too, raising dust. We're breathing it right now. What's wrong? Choking? Here, have a sip of water.

Better now? Where were we . . . oh, yeah. The manure goes into vast "lagoons," acres and acres wide. If you're unlucky enough to live anywhere nearby, the stench is unbelievable. It's giving off hundreds of gases, many of them poisonous. A sample:

- **Hydrogen sulfide:** Smells like rotten eggs. Many farmers think if they can't smell it, then they're safe. Actually, when it's strong enough, hydrogen sulfide paralyzes the nerve cells of the nose. So the farmer leans over the edge, takes a whiff, doesn't smell anything . . . then passes out and tumbles into the lagoon.
- **Ammonia:** Smells like drying pee. When it gets into the air, it adds to "fine particulate pollution" (tiny bits of stuff floating around—not good for asthma) and helps cause acid rain. Seventy percent of the ammonia in our air comes from factory farms.
- **Carbon dioxide:** No smell at all. A stealth gas—and a greenhouse gas, too. If the FBI put up WANTED posters for global warming, the face of CO_2 would be in every post office across America. We dump a billion tons of it into the atmosphere every few weeks, and those lagoons aren't helping.
- **Methane:** Cow burps, cow farts, and cow poop may sound funny, but the cloud of poison coming out of all those burping, farting, pooping cows isn't so amusing. Thanks largely to methane, livestock generate more greenhouse gases than all the motorcycles, cars, trucks, buses, trains, ships, and airplanes in the world.

That's air pollution. Then there's water. Lagoons often leak or burst or overflow. When they do, the raw sewage runs off into the nearest stream or river, killing fish and contaminating the local drinking water. (Like that refreshing sip of water you just took.) But water doesn't stay local. Eventually, it makes its way to the sea. There, the runoff helps create enormous "dead zones" where practically nothing can live. One

*Growing, processing, and shipping food now sucks up as much energy as our homes and cars.

dead zone off the Gulf Coast is nearly the size of New Jersey.

Now here's the crazy part. Traditionally, on a farm, cow manure is not a problem. In fact, it's *good*. The cows wander around the field, eating grass and pooping it back out. By doing that, they're spreading grass seed, along with natural fertilizer to help it grow. In other words, they're replanting their own food source as they go. Pretty slick, huh? (Okay, maybe that wasn't the best choice of words.)

FAST FORWARD

Does quick have to mean dirty? Not if you ask Chipotle, Burgerville, or Pizza Fusion. These fast-food chains are known for using fresh, organic, and/or hormone-free ingredients, often from local farms. At Burgerville, you only get to order onion rings if Walla Walla onions are in season; the same goes for strawberry shakes. Word is, it's worth the wait.

On a factory farm, cows don't eat grass. They eat corn. Now, "corn-fed" sounds healthy and tasty, doesn't it? Really, though, feeding corn to cows is about as healthy as feeding donuts to your dog. Cows aren't meant to eat corn, and it makes them sick. Plus, the corn is sprayed with lots of chemicals—bug killer, weed killer, synthetic fertilizers made out of petroleum. Some of that stuff stays in the cow, ending up in your fast-food burger or filet mignon. And some of it comes out the other end, turning nature's fertilizer into toxic waste for cows to wallow in.

To keep the cows from keeling over before they're full-grown, farmers put antibiotics in their feed—just like the antibiotics we take when we're sick. But for years, people have been taking antibiotics way too often. Doctors are now much more careful to prescribe them only when they're really needed. Why? Because overusing them gives antibiotic-resistant bacteria a chance to develop, creating deadly new diseases with no cure.

Unfortunately, while doctors have cut down on the use of antibiotics, factory farms have not. Compared to humans, livestock use *more than five times* as many antibiotics. They wouldn't need these drugs if they were out in a field munching grass, the way they're meant to do, instead of getting stuffed with feedlot corn.

And feeding corn to cows doesn't just make the cows sick. It helps make people sick, too. People and cows have different kinds of stomachs. Our stomachs have more acid. This used to keep us fairly safe from food poisoning if harmful *E. coli* microbes got into our meat. But if we feed corn (people food) to cows, their digestive systems become more like ours. *E. coli* strains bred in a feedlot cow are better at surviving in a human stomach. Terrific news for the *E. coli*. Not so great for us.

Now, you probably don't eat a lot of cow guts—at least, not as far as you know. So why should you worry about *E. coli*?

Well, this is where it gets a little gross.

E. coli lives in cow poop. So do cows. They stand in it, and lie in it, and it gets caked onto their hides. They have it on the inside, too, of course, in their intestines.

When the cows get to the slaughterhouse, the workers are supposed to make sure no manure falls in the meat. But when a side of beef swings past every ten seconds, and knife-wielding workers have to keep up with the frantic pace or lose their (low-paid) jobs, hygiene may not be the first thing on their minds.

Hang on. Aren't there regulations or inspectors or anything?

A few. But four giant meatpacking companies control 80 percent of the industry. They have a lot of influence. (Read: money.) And if you're thinking they might use that influence to keep from getting regulated and inspected any more than they would like to be—well, let's just say you're not alone.

The USDA is the government agency in charge of keeping our meat poop-free. Say the USDA finds out that a slaughterhouse is filthy and the meat's contaminated. Does it close down the plant? Does it recall the meat? Does it issue a big fat fine?

Nope. It doesn't have the power. All it is allowed to do is "consult" with the company about what it should do . . . please . . . that is, if you'd like to, sir.

HOW LOW CAN THEY GO?

In the winter of 2009, eight people died and thousands more got sick from tainted peanut butter. A tragic accident? Well, not exactly. As reported by *The Washington Post* and *The New York Times*, the people at the company knew there was *salmonella* in the peanut butter. But they went ahead and sold it anyway, for years. How did they get away with it so long? Simple. By law, they were allowed to keep their test results a secret—from state regulators, from the U.S. government, and, of course, from us.

One cow with *E. coli* can infect 32,000 pounds of ground beef. That's 128,000 people puking up their guts—or worse—because they ate a quarter pounder.

If the workers didn't have to slice and dice so fast, they might be able to keep the manure out of the meat. But speed is money for the meatpackers. So they zap the meat with radiation: X-rays, gamma rays, electron beams. Irradiation kills bacteria. It also rips the meat apart at the molecular level, destroying its nutrition, creating toxic chemicals, and making it taste funny.

And, of course, you're still eating cow poop. But now it's *irradiated* cow poop.

So: Weed-killer in your burger. Anti-biotic-resistant superbugs. *E. coli* poisoning. If all these problems start with feeding corn to cows . . . why is anybody doing it?

Follow the money. Like cotton (and unlike, for instance, peas and carrots), corn is heavily subsidized. The U.S. government pays farmers to grow corn. The more they grow, the more money they get. So there's a lot of corn out there.

A *lot* of corn.

Mountains of corn. Corn overflowing giant concrete silos in town after town across the Midwest. Fields of corn stretching so far they can be seen from outer space.

CHANGE THE GAME

Hey! Let's give a lot of money to the biggest, richest farmers so that they can grow some more of what there's already too much of, using chemicals that make us sick. Sounds crazy? That's because it is. Let's tell Congress to make our next farm bill pay for what we *want: healthy food, healthy communities, and healthy farms.*

It isn't good corn. The people who grow it hardly ever touch the stuff themselves. ("We're growing crap," one Iowa farmer grumbles in the documentary *King Corn*. "Poorest quality crap the world has ever seen.")

But, thanks to Uncle Sam, there's plenty of it. And it has to be used up.

To make a pound of factory-farmed beef, a cow needs to eat ten pounds of corn. In other words, two and a half pounds of corn go into the meat in that quarter pounder! But that's just for starters.

Pull out a few boxes from your kitchen cabinet and take a look at the ingredients. See any of these?

MODIFIED CORN STARCH · MALTODEXTRIN · LECITHIN · HIGH-FRUCTOSE CORN SYRUP · DEXTROSE · CARAMEL COLOR · XANTHAN GUM · HYDROLYZED CORN PROTEIN · CORN GLUTEN · CORNSTARCH · MSG · LACTIC ACID · LYSINE · CORN FLOUR · ASCORBIC ACID

It's all corn.

More than a quarter of the items in the supermarket contain corn. And fast food is even cornier. As Michael Pollan points out in his book *The Omnivore's Dilemma*, just about anything you can order at McDonald's will have corn in it: The fries (corn oil). The burger (corn fed). Even the buns, the ketchup, and the salad dressing include corn syrup—not to mention the soda. And when Pollan picked up a McDonald's flyer to see what was in his son's Chicken McNuggets, he counted thirteen ingredients that came from corn.

So what? Corn's pretty good for you, right?

Corn on the cob, sure. It's got complex carbohydrates, protein, fiber, vitamins, and minerals. Corn processed into high-fructose corn syrup hasn't got any of that stuff, though. It's pure sugar. There's no nutrition in all the additives made out of corn, either. And corn-fed beef is extra high in saturated fat.

Grab a Big Mac (540 calories, 45 grams of fat), large fries (500 calories, 25 grams of fat), and a 32-ounce Coke (310 calories and the equivalent of more than 21 teaspoons of sugar), and you've got the perfect meal to make you unhealthy and overweight.

Ask Jazlyn and Ashley, the two girls who sued McDonald's for making them fat. Like a lot of kids their age, they ate there all the time. (One in three kids in America eats fast food every day.) And like a lot of kids their age, they got big. (Since your parents were young, the number of overweight teenagers in the United States has *tripled*.)

McDonald's lawyers told the judge that everybody knows fast food is bad for you. So even though they fork out billions on TV ads to get kids and teens to buy their food—and though nutrition information wasn't posted where customers were likely to spot it—Jazlyn and Ashley should have just said no.

Case dismissed. And soon after, under pressure from the food industry, lawmakers around the country rushed through "cheeseburger bills" making it illegal to sue fast food restaurants if you get fat.

The star and filmmaker of *Super Size Me*, Morgan Spurlock, wanted to see what would happen if he ate nothing but McDonald's for a month. He was thin and healthy, so a team of doctors gave him the okay.

In the first twelve days, he gained seventeen pounds. By the third week, his head pounded, he had chest pains, and he could barely make it up the stairs. His girlfriend and his mom were freaking out. So were the doctors. They couldn't believe fast food could make someone so sick, so quick. They told him if he kept it up, he'd die of liver failure.

Kind of makes you want to dial 9-1-1 at the sight of a French fry, doesn't it?

Before you grab that cell phone, though, read this. . . .

MORE

- "Take the red pill, and I'll show you the truth," intones the cartoon cow in the dark suit and shades. Watch *The Meatrix Trilogy* online at meatrix.com. More fun than you ever thought a slaughterhouse could be!
- *Chew on This: Everything You Don't Want to Know About Fast Food*—really, the title says it all. It's the teen-friendly spin-off of Eric Schlosser's bestselling book *Fast Food Nation*.
- *McLibel: The Story of Two People Who Wouldn't Say McSorry* is a documentary movie about two protestors who stood up when the fast-food giant tried to shut them down.

Chapter 5

TRASH TALK

Your cell phone's secret life.

What's the scariest thing in *your* cell phone?

(a) The Crazy Frog ringtone?

(b) A video of your best friend's brother giving himself a swirly?

(c) Snoopware that lets your parents peek at what you're texting? (Luckily, they have no clue what you could mean by "CTN POS G2G.")

ow about BFRs?

No, that's not textspeak. It stands for "brominated flame retardants"—chemicals meant to keep your cell phone (and your head) from bursting into flames. Unfortunately, that's not all they do. Every time you pull your phone out of your pocket, itty-bitty bits of toxic BFRs flake off and float away . . . except for those you breathe in. Guess who has more of this stuff in their blood than anyone else tested in the world? American kids.

How about mercury and lead?

These heavy metals are so poisonous, even tiny amounts are a serious threat. As journalist Elizabeth Royte points out in her book *Garbage Land: On the Secret Trail of Trash*, "One Sweet Tart-sized mercury battery is enough to put a six-ton load of garbage over the fed's allowable limit for solid waste." But there is mercury in cell phones, and lead, too. Researchers who tested cell phones found more lead in most of them than U.S. safety standards allow. And those standards may not count for much. Doctors now say that even "safe" levels of lead in kids' bodies can lower their IQ.

Actually, cell phones are so chock-full of toxics, it's tough to pick the scariest. That sleek little gadget in your hand may contain dozens of dangerous chemicals, from PCBs to PVC, from arsenic to zinc. See for yourself. Check the list of ingredients.

Oh, that's right. It didn't *come* with a list of ingredients, did it?

Electronics companies won't tell you exactly what they put in your cell phone, TV, music player, or computer. They may not even know. After all, what they use in their factories comes from hundreds, even thousands, of other factories all around the world. And those factories churn out brand-new chemical concoctions almost every day.

CHANGE THE GAME

Nutrition labels help us tell real fruit juice from Kool-Aid. But even things we don't eat or drink can affect our health. Why shouldn't we require companies to tell us what's in everything we buy?

Happily, most of the ickiness is tucked away inside your cell phone's plastic shell. That means you're probably okay, as long as you don't smash it, mash it, fry it up, and dunk it in a glass of water that you plan to drink.

So, what's the problem, then? How many cell phones does *that* happen to?

Oh . . . about a hundred million.

At least, that's how many phones get thrown away each year in the United States, where people typically buy a phone, use it a year or so, then toss it in the trash as soon as a trendy new model hits the stores.

The trouble with throwing things "away" is that there's no such place. Though we may think our phones lie buried and forgotten in the dump, the deadly chemicals inside are rising like a zombie army from the grave to stalk the land.

Picture what happens at a landfill. A garbage truck rolls in. It dumps its load. Giant machines roll over the day's trash, crushing it down and making space for more. Deep in the pile, a shattered cell phone spills its guts.

Rain falls. It seeps into the trash, soaking up anything it finds along the way: putrid banana, spoiled milk, nail polish, bleach, cigarette butts, the toxics in the phone. This poisonous juice trickles to the bottom, where a plastic liner holds it— for a while.

Like all landfills, though, sooner or later this one springs a leak. And all that nasty stuff we threw "away" spreads gradually through the groundwater . . . until, one day, it pops up in our drinking source. Surprise!

While liquids dribble from the bottom of the dump, gases bubble out the top.

Garbage breaking down belches out methane and carbon dioxide—greenhouse gases. Often, these are laced with cancer-causing chemicals picked up from items in the trash. (*Cough*—cell phone?—*cough*.)

The action isn't over when the trash quits coming, either. Way back in the 1970s, somebody got a bright idea about what to do with all those useless closed-down dumps: Throw a bunch of dirt on top, scatter some grass seed, and voilà! You've got a nice new playground, sledding hill, or park.

Only, weird things kept happening. Used syringes poked up like spring flowers. Patches of mud appeared that smelled like rotten eggs and snapped, crackled, and popped like a bowl of Rice Krispies. In 1995, in Charlotte, North Carolina, a mom ran to pick up a soccer ball when it fell in a hole. To help her see, she flicked her lighter. *WHOOMPH!* A methane fireball exploded, blowing her right off her feet.

FAST FORWARD

Trash or treasure? The methane gas let off by decomposing garbage can be captured and used as a source of energy, and many landfills are now doing just that. Of course, we want to throw out *less*, not more, so we shouldn't plan to get all our power from piles of garbage.

Of course, not all our trash goes to a landfill. Some is burned in an incinerator, spewing chemicals and cooking up dioxin,

the most toxic human-made substance on earth. Whatever doesn't waft away falls down as ash, and *that* gets taken . . . to the dump.

But maybe you would never throw a cell phone (or a TV, or a Nintendo console, or an iPod) in the garbage. Maybe you realize that a tidal wave of toxic "e-waste"—the United Nations says it totals *fifty million tons a year* worldwide—is breaking over our heads. Maybe you're one of the few, the proud, the dedicated 12.5 percent of Americans who bring in their old unwanted electronics for recycling.

That 12.5 percent was out in force at a recycling drive in Denver, Colorado. The cars lined up bumper-to-bumper. Families waited patiently for hours to place their e-waste in safe hands.

A *60 Minutes* TV crew tracked the collected electronics to see where they went. Would they be fixed up for schools that couldn't afford new ones? Or would they go to a state-of-the-art recycling plant, to be transformed into the latest high-tech wonder?

Not even close.

The TV crew ended up in Guiyu, a town in southern China. Guiyu didn't look much like a town. It looked like a gigantic garbage dump. Little kids played on heaps of broken, burned-out TVs and computers, while their mothers melted circuit boards over coal fires, sending up clouds of deadly smoke. Guiyu hunkered at the edge of a brown, stinking river, scrubbing clothes as twisted chunks of plastic floated by.

Halfway around the world in Ghana, West Africa, it's the same grim scene: piles of smashed electronics, plumes of foul smoke, teenage boys leaning over toxic barbecues, choking as they roast the plastic coating off a dollar's worth of copper wire.

This is where most of the e-waste we recycle goes: to ruined towns in Ghana, Nigeria, India, Pakistan, Bangladesh, Malaysia, China, Vietnam—anywhere safety and environmental rules are lax, and people are too desperately poor to say no to the "bads" (not goods) we throw away.

REBELS WITH A CAUSE

Teenager Alex Lin of Westerly, Rhode Island, was eleven when he first read a news story about e-waste. He'd never heard of the problem before, but, he says, "I thought we could do something about it." So he did. He got some friends together and formed the Westerly Innovations Network (WIN), collecting used computers and fixing them up for people who needed them. Today, WIN computers are in use as far away as Mexico, Sri Lanka, and Cameroon.

But once again, it turns out there is no "away." Polluted air crosses the ocean, carrying our killer chemicals right back to us. And when we buy cheap necklaces and key chains made in China, then find out that they're full of lead, why should we be shocked? The materials have been "recycled" from our old cell phones and computers.

Cleaner, safer ways of dealing with our e-waste do exist, and if you take your old cell phone in for recycling, there's one chance in ten it will get to a modern high-tech plant. (No, those aren't the greatest odds.)

But unless your new phone is made of nothing but cleanly recycled materials— and the chance of *that* is roughly zilch— you're creating more trash than you've saved. In fact, recycling a phone and then buying a new one is like plucking one littered candy wrapper from the grass . . . then turning around and unloading a whole Dumpster's worth in the same spot.

Check it out:

- The eensy-weensy spider threads of gold used in a cell phone's circuit board leave behind 220 pounds of waste.
- Think that old desktop computer at the back of your classroom looks heavy? The raw materials it took to make it weighed nearly two tons.
- Nearly half the toxic waste in the United States comes from a single industry— mining. Every year, mines churn out nine times more waste than all the garbage

trucks pick up in every town and city in the nation.

Most metals come from huge open-pit mines. "Open-pit" means exactly what it sounds like—an enormous hole ripped in the ground. (The biggest one, Bingham Canyon in Utah, is a mile deep and two and a half miles across.)

Here's what happens at a gold mine. First, machines scoop out the dirt and rock and dump it in a giant pile. Then, they spray cyanide on it to make the gold separate out. A dose of cyanide no bigger than a grain of rice can kill you. Mines use *tons* of it a day.

But that's not the only poison in the rubble. Arsenic, cadmium, mercury, and lead are in there, too—along with pyrite, also known as "fool's gold." When air and water hit the pyrite, it creates sulfuric acid. Groundwater near mines can be *ten thousand times more acidic than battery acid.*

Out of all the rubble, 0.00001 percent is gold. The other 99.99999 percent is waste, left behind in piles that reach thirty stories high.

It doesn't have to be like this. There's another way, "above-ground mining," which could net billions of dollars in gold, silver, copper, palladium, and platinum. Above-ground mining uses just a fraction of the energy and resources sucked up by an ordinary mine, and is much less harmful to the earth and our health. And it pays. Per ton, compared to what is dug out of open-pit mines, above-ground ore yields two hundred times as much gold.

Have you guessed? "Above-ground mining" means recycling.

Metals are extremely easy to reuse. Copper, for instance, is completely recyclable. And recycled electronics could provide all the gold needed for every cell phone in the world, without digging up so much as a spoonful more.

FAST FORWARD

The hardest thing about electronics recycling is prying out all the different materials. But what if cell phones took *themselves* apart to be recycled? Nokia made a model phone that pops apart in just two seconds. Using "shape memory," screws straighten out and springs expand, pushing open the plastic case and setting free the circuit board. It only works at 140° to 300°F, so it can't fall to pieces in your pocket. When will it be on the market? Why not call up Nokia and ask?

Instead, we dump precious metals by the ton into our landfills and incinerators, and the mining industry keeps chugging right along. Why? Because it's cheaper to dig up new metals than recycle old ones—thanks to Uncle Sam.

Under the Mining Act of 1872 (no, that is not a typo: *eighteen* seventy-two), mining companies pay only five dollars an acre to rip up our public land, keep every penny for themselves, and leave us to clean up the mess. In big business, this is called "externalizing costs."

Externalize means "put outside." (As in, "Dad, I just externalized the dog.") When you externalize a cost, you put it outside of your business by not paying for it—which is to say, you get somebody else to foot the bill.

Say a little kid sets up a lemonade stand. His doting mom buys him lemons and sugar. She gives him a stack of plastic cups. She lets him use a pitcher. She even mops up when he spills sticky lemonade all over her clean kitchen floor.

Then the kid carries the lemonade out to the sidewalk, sells it at fifty cents a cup, and pockets all the money.

That's externalizing costs.

Now say the kid becomes insanely rich selling millions of gallons of lemonade. And he makes the lemonade with toxic chemicals—overflowing vats of toxic chemicals, spilling out everywhere, poisoning the whole neighborhood....

Sound ridiculous? Maybe not if you live in Mountain View, California, a town sickened by greed and LUST ... that is, Leaking Underground Storage Tanks, full of cancer-causing chemicals used to make microchips for electronics such as cell phones.

Turn on the tap in Mountain View, and you get water piped from 175 miles away. At one point, as Elizabeth Grossman tells it in her book *High Tech Trash*, the Environmental Protection Agency told the people here

that it would be three hundred years before their own water was safe to drink.

How do the big corporations get away with this? Shouldn't there be a law?

There are laws. Pretty good ones, too. Laws that make electronics companies responsible for taking back and recycling their e-waste. Laws that stop them from putting toxic ingredients like lead and mercury and BFRs into their products in the first place. Laws that say they need to prove the chemicals they use are safe.

So you're all set ... that is, if you happen to live in Europe, where the laws were passed. If you live in the United States, though, it's a different story.

Ninety-five percent of all the chemicals in the United States haven't been tested. At least, they haven't been tested in a lab for their effect on people and the environment. But they are being tested every day on millions of unpaid, clueless human guinea pigs, also known as the American consumer.

European laws are based on the "precautionary principle." This is the idea that if you think something might be causing serious and irreversible damage, you should stop. Common sense, right?

Not in the United States. To ban a chemical, the EPA has to show not just compelling evidence of harm but *proof*. This can take decades. And in the meantime, companies are free to keep pouring the stuff into their products. (Not to mention our air and water.)

One reason why it's hard to pin down the

effect of one specific chemical is that there are so many out there. If people are exposed to lots of chemicals, and they get sick, how can we tell which one it was? In fact, that mix may be the biggest unknown danger. As any kid who's ever played with a chemistry set knows, a chemical can be perfectly harmless on its own. But throw in one or two others, and—*BANG!*

Even when it manages to prove a chemical is harmful, the EPA can't just say no. It has to weigh the "costs to industry" and come up with a rule that is "least burdensome." In other words, our right not to be poisoned is balanced against the companies' right to make obscene amounts of money selling us dangerous stuff.

In close to forty years, out of more than sixty thousand chemicals on the market, the EPA banned a grand total of . . .

(Drum roll, please.)

Five.

As one government official smugly put it, " . . . we do not recognize any universal precautionary principle. We consider it to be a mythical concept, perhaps like a unicorn."

Right. Dream on, dude.

But all across America, cell phones are ringing.

It's a wake-up call.

MORE

- Lots of places will take your old cell phone for recycling. GreenPhone.com pays you for it, and covers the postage, too. They even plant a tree for every phone they buy.
- Nancy Farmer's novel *The Ear, the Eye and the Arm* takes you to a future Africa, where mutant kids mine toxic dumps for plastic—and the weird part is, it's actually fun to read.
- Get the latest on e-waste from the Electronics TakeBack Coalition at electronicstakeback.com.

Chapter 6

SO LONG, FRANKENFOODS

To organic . . . and beyond!

Amelia Bloomer	P. T. Barnum	Joan of Arc
Harriet Tubman	Blackbeard	Socrates
Pocahontas	Jesse James	Confucius
Attila the Hun	Sitting Bull	King Arthur
Ivan the Terrible	Cleopatra	William Shakespeare

Here's a fun fact: All these famous people grew up eating 100 percent organically grown food.

Okay, *everybody* ate organic food. Only they didn't call it "organic" back then. They just called it . . . food.

The big change came in the late 1940s, after World War II. During the war, American factories churned out the bomb-making chemical ammonium nitrate by the ton. Then the fighting stopped, and nobody knew what to do with all the leftover nitrate—until somebody pointed out that it was just like the stuff that made cow pies and chicken droppings such good fertilizer. So instead of dropping chemical nitrate on foreign cities, why not spread it on our fields?

Meanwhile, over in Germany, the Nazis had invented a new type of insecticide. To their delight, these chemicals, organophosphates, weren't just good for killing bugs. They were also great at killing people—so great that, as "nerve agents," they've since been declared illegal weapons under international law. As "insecticides," however, they're still sprayed on everything from rice paddies to cotton fields to apple trees.

Words are funny things. Take the word *conventional*, meaning regular, ordinary. It's become "conventional" to drench crops in poison, pump up baby cows with 'roids, and shoot bananas with a gamma ray so that they don't get all mushy on their 2,500-mile trip from South America. Thanks to all this, we need a special name for what used to be plain old ordinary food: "organic."

Now, we could go on for hours about why food grown without a bunch of toxic chemicals is better for our bodies and the earth. But really... duh.

NO WAY!

Can just *breathing* make you fat? Maybe. Japanese scientists discovered that tributyltin, a common pesticide, can slow the metabolism and turn on the "fat" genes. And you don't even have to eat food that's been sprayed. Like other pesticides, tributyltin is widespread in the environment. The good news? Growing all our food organically could take a load not only off our minds, but also our behinds!

Recently, a team of scientists let lab rats choose between two kinds of biscuits—one made of organic wheat, the other not. The rats went straight for the organic.

Most people are at least as smart as rats. They would rather eat non-toxic food. So, why isn't everyone eating organic?

Ask, and you might hear something like this:

Organic is okay for latte-sipping yuppie snobs, but my family can't afford it.

Amen to that! Organic food *is* too expensive. Or maybe it's the other food that's just too cheap.

Too cheap? How can that be?

Of course, not many people gripe because the things they buy don't cost enough. But sometimes things that *look* cheap really aren't so cheap at all.

Say you're walking down a city sidewalk, and you see a folding table piled high with your favorite video games. A big sign says SALE—99¢.

Wow! What a bargain! Thrilled, you buy some games and head on home to play. But when you load the first game into your console, it doesn't work. You try them all. Worthless. And worse—*all* your money's gone! While you were drooling over his table, the salesman's accomplice picked your pocket.

Factory-farmed food doesn't work, either. It doesn't do what food's supposed to do: taste good and be good for you. Chicken doesn't taste like chicken without added "chicken flavor." The supermarket jets in strawberries year-round, but they're not sweet. And, compared to the fresh vegetables your grandparents grew up on, the ones we eat today have fewer vitamins and minerals. That means you have to eat *more* broccoli, brussels sprouts, and spinach to get the same boost. Talk about unfair.

And while the food companies wave their 99¢ signs in our faces, they're reaching around to pick our back pockets. Remember subsidies, free money from the government for the toxic "cides" and "izers" that are poisoning our food? And externalizing, that neat trick of getting *us* to mop up all those cides and izers when they spill into our water and our air and make us sick?

So what? you may be thinking. *I don't pay for that.*

Sure, you don't see those costs at the cash register. But you're paying—with your health, your future, and the billions of tax dollars that could be spent on something better than bad food.

Maybe it's the skate park your town can't afford to build. Or the art and music programs they've cut from your school. Or a local farmer who would love to get a subsidy to bring you fresh, organic produce at a lower price.

Yeah, yeah, but organic food does *cost more at the store.*

True. Luckily, most of us can pay for it with what we save not buying useless junk like bottled tap water or a new cell phone when the old one works just fine.

REBELS WITH A CAUSE

Is organic really that expensive? Salon.com writer Siobhan Phillips decided to find out. Shopping on a food-stamp budget, she went **SOLE** (sustainable, organic, local, and/or ethical) for a whole month. It hurt to give up Cheerios and pepperoni pizza, she reports. But homemade chili, oatmeal sprinkled with cinnamon sugar, and organic peanut butter slathered on a slice of fresh-baked bread helped ease the pain.

Out of every dollar American families spend, less than ten cents goes for food. And almost half of that ten cents is spent eating out, which costs more than cooking at home. These days, Americans spend less of their money on food than they ever have before—probably less than *anybody* ever has before.

Wake up, people! Nothing we buy is more important than the food we swallow. It's time for a serious attitude change.

But what about people who really can't afford to buy organic food—or any food? What about all those starving kids in Africa?

Organic is okay for latte-sipping yuppie snobs, but it won't feed the world.

- -

Back in the 1980s, the singer Thomas Dolby had a popular music video on MTV. It took place at the "Home for Deranged

Scientists," and featured a wild-eyed old man waving his arms and roaring, "*Science!*"

That's pretty much how biotech companies react when anyone mentions organics. Pointing to the millions of hungry people in the world and our soaring population growth, they claim the only way we possibly can feed everyone is—*science!*

Well, there's good science. There's bad science. And then there's weird science.

The science touted by the biotech folks is "genetic engineering" (also called GE). GE uses "cell invasion technology" to blast viruses into the cells of plants and animals. The viruses infect the plants and animals with the genes of other, unrelated species, turning them into genetically modified organisms, or GMOs. Some people call them "Frankenfoods."

A toxic bug-killing potato, registered as a pesticide, but sold as food. (*Science!*)

A pig crossed with a jellyfish to make it glow in the dark. (*Science!*)

GMOs may sound like something from a freaky sci-fi movie, but they're real—and they're everywhere. Roll a shopping cart up any supermarket aisle, throw ten items in the cart, and chances are, seven of them will have genetically modified ingredients.

They won't be labeled, either. Ever since the first GE tomato flopped in 1994, biotech has fought tooth and nail to keep Americans from finding out what's in our food. After all, if shoppers knew which foods were tampered with, we might not buy them. Plus, if people started getting sick, it could be traced back to the source.

ACT OUT!

Demand to know what's in your food! Call your representative and senators and ask them nicely to get off their butts and pass the Genetically Engineered Food Right to Know Act. Thecampaign.org will even give you tips on what to say.

No one's ever proved genetically modified food is safe to eat. In fact, it may cause problems ranging from severe food allergies to antibiotic resistance to mutations. But the really scary thing about GE is that it's already out of control.

In nature, pigs don't mate with jellyfish and spawn glow-in-the-dark jellypigs. But seeds from one field of corn or canola do float into other fields of the same crop. There, they cross-pollinate and breed.

In the movie *The Future of Food*, family farmers talk about their fields being contaminated by a GE seed sold by the biotech giant Monsanto. Did Monsanto apologize? Pay for a cleanup? No. Instead, the farmers say, the company threatened to sue them if they didn't pay to use the genes they "stole."

Biotech companies are not about feeding the world. They're about the moola. For years, they've been working on a "terminator gene" that makes a seed destroy itself.

That way, instead of saving seeds from each year's crop and planting them next season, as they have always done, farmers would be forced to buy more seeds.

Maybe that's only fair. If a company develops a special, new, improved variety, the farmer shouldn't use it without paying, right?

But what if other plants pick up the terminator gene?

Suppose one plant in a thousand isn't sterile. Instead, it's a carrier of the gene. The wind blows its pollen to another field . . . birds spread the seed. . . .

Imagine: All the world's crops committing suicide. Empty grocery shelves. Barren fields. Desperate farmers paying their last penny for the only seeds that grow— labeled PROPERTY OF BIG BRAND X.

FAST FORWARD

What's the opposite of suicide food? Crops that thrive without chemicals—or any human help. At The Land Institute in Salina, Kansas, they've been crossing grains with wild grasses and sowing the seeds with other kinds of plants. The goal? A farm that works just like a prairie, growing strong and tall on nothing but sunshine and rain year after year.

Biotech companies paint a prettier picture of the GE future. They promise bigger, better, more nutritious food. Children rescued from starvation and disease. Toxic pesticides and herbicides replaced by "clean" genetically engineered solutions.

Is it possible? Who knows? So far, their track record is pretty sad.

GE crops have actually driven pesticide use *up*, not down, by millions of pounds. And they've created "superweeds" that thrive no matter how much they are sprayed.

In Kenya, a genetically modified sweet potato plant came out with great fanfare. The end of hunger! No more poverty! But there weren't any press conferences and photo ops a few years later, when backers quietly admitted that the Franken-spuds had *lower* yields than ordinary sweet potatoes.

In India, thousands of farmers went deep into debt to buy the new GMO seeds, and then watched their crops fail. Losing all hope, the farmers killed themselves by swallowing the pesticides they had been told they would no longer need.

Meanwhile, in southeast Asian rain forests, on north Africa's tropical savannah, and in the Andes mountains of South America, organic farmers have been harvesting nearly twice as much food as their neighbors. In fact, in study after study, it turns out that in the poorest countries, farmers can *triple* what they grow just by going organic.

Surprise!

Now, in rich countries like the United States and Canada, organic yields are slightly lower. But we already have too much food. The USDA reports that of all the food we grow in the United States, more than a quarter of it gets tossed out. That's enough to feed all the hungry kids in the world—and their families—twice over.

Is that a hand waving back there? Yes? Speak up, please.

Organic is okay, but . . . is there anything better?

Ah. Yes.

Once again . . . words are funny things.

For a long time, the only folks who grew organic food were true believers. Rather than fight nature, they worked with it— letting animals have grass and sunshine, planting a mix of crops to naturally fend off pests, feeding and caring for the soil. Nothing was wasted; everything had a use.

At first, everyone laughed at their foolish notions. Why go to all that extra work? But slowly, news leaked out that all was not well in the land of amber waves of grain. Farmers who sprayed their fields refused to eat the crops they grew. "Food scares" took over the nightly news with outbreaks of food poisoning from chicken, eggs, beef, cheese, and even strawberries, orange juice, lettuce, and tomatoes. People started to look for a different kind of food, one that didn't come sealed up in plastic, stamped with bar codes, or shoved out of a drive-up window in a paper sack.

Now that this organic thing was taking

off, the industrial food giants wanted in. From there, it was a hop, skip, and a jump to regulation.

Here's the good thing about regulation: the government controls the word *organic*. That means companies who claim to be selling organic food have to back up their claim. When you see the USDA organic seal, you can be fairly sure that whatever it's on meets the official standards.

Here's the bad thing about regulation: the government controls the word *organic*. And with the food industry spending millions on lobbyists who fly to Washington, D.C., take lawmakers out to fancy restaurants, and tell them what laws they should pass . . . well, those official standards tend to slide.

That's what Americans found out in 1997, when the USDA unveiled its first draft of organic standards. The USDA planned to let food be labeled "organic" even if it was genetically modified, irradiated, and grown in (hold your breath) *sewage sludge*.

Sewage sludge isn't just straight poop. It's whatever gets poured down the drain, not just in homes but also factories. A lot of it is toxic. Some of it is even radioactive. Cows have died from eating hay grown in fields "fertilized" with this sludge.

Americans flipped out.

Swamped with more than 275,000 outraged phone calls, letters, and e-mails demanding *real* organic standards, the USDA backed down.

Today, "organic" means that—unlike the rest of the food in the supermarket—your food is free of sewage sludge, irradiation, GMOs, chemical pesticides and fertilizers, hormones, and antibiotics. And that's all good.

But is it good enough?

The thing about the mega-companies doing organic is . . . they just don't *get* it.

They cram cows by the thousands into "organic feedlots" and stuff them with—guess what?—organic corn.

They raise lettuce on vast "organic farms"—millions of pounds of it a week—then seal it in miles of plastic, pump it full of gas to keep it "fresh," and ship it across the country in refrigerated trucks.

They process food into "organic" TV dinners spiked with chemical additives. (Yep, there go those government standards again, slip-slidin' away.)

Now, even Big Organic is a step in the right direction. When Wal-Mart stocks organic food on the shelves of thousands of superstores, that means a lot of farmland is no longer getting soaked in chemicals. Definitely a plus.

But we can do much, much better.

These days, a lot of the best farmers in America don't call themselves organic. Some of them don't want to spend their time filling out piles of forms instead of farming. Some of them can't pony up the big bucks for the USDA label. And some just think the word *organic* has been chewed and popped and chewed again until it's lost its flavor. Instead, they use words like *humane*, *sustainable*, even *beyond organic*.

And then there's a Virginia farmer named Joel Salatin, who calls himself a "Christian libertarian environmentalist capitalist." It's a little too long to fit on a sign. So, instead, he put one up that said, JOEL SALATIN: LUNATIC FARMER.

One of Salatin's crazy ideas is that animals should do what makes them happy. Chickens, for instance. What they like to do is scratch. So Salatin built them a chicken house on wheels, which he calls the Eggmobile. Now they follow along after the cows, scratching through the cow patties and pecking out the grubs and fly eggs that they find. (No, it wouldn't make *you* happy, but you're not a chicken.)

No antibiotics needed: the chickens eat the bugs that could make the cows sick. No chemical fertilizer needed: the chickens spread the cow-poop fertilizer on the field, and add their own. The cows are happy. The chickens are happy. And the farmer's happy, because he can sell the healthiest, best-tasting eggs and beef for miles around.

On his farm, Salatin says, the animals do most of the work. Cows mow the fields. Chickens clean up after the rabbits. And pigs, rooting for corn, fluff up the compost with their snouts. These jobs respect the basic nature of each animal—what Salatin calls the "chickenness" of the chicken and the "pigness" of the pig.

But here's the most exciting part:

His farm uses technology that collects free solar energy, adds vitamins to meat, and, best of all, actually sucks harmful greenhouse gases right out of the atmosphere.

The name of this technology is . . . grass.

No joke! Carefully managed pastures really can pull carbon from the atmosphere and put it in the soil, where instead of causing global warming, it helps more grass grow. This is known as "carbon farming."

A single acre can take in 7,000 pounds of carbon dioxide a year. If every farmer in America turned to such methods, some scientists say, it would be like making half the nation's cars vanish into thin air.

Salatin goes further. He claims that if every farmer in the world farmed his way, it would take less than ten years to clean up all the carbon that's been puffed into the sky since the Industrial Revolution.

Ordering a burger "your way"? Maybe that should mean it's made of grass-fed beef.

Of course, that doesn't work so well if the burger has traveled 2500 miles in a fuel-guzzling, carbon-dioxide-belching reefer truck before it gets slapped on your plate.

Yes, the system is insane. But don't go loco.

Just go local.

MORE

- They're young. They're hip. They're funny. And they're heading out to Iowa to grow some corn. Pop in the *King Corn* DVD, pull up a couch and grab a bag of corn chips—it may be your last.

- If you're thinking about eating, well, pretty much anything, the latest scoop is at the Center for Food Safety (centerforfoodsafety.org).

- Michael Pollan's bestseller *The Omnivore's Dilemma* is now out in an edition for young readers. Find out what's *really* for dinner.

- Roasted guinea pig? Polar bear steaks? Sea horses on a stick? For their book *What the World Eats*, Faith D'Aluisio and Peter Menzel visited twenty-five families around the world and peeked into their cooking pots. Amazing photos, and serious food for thought.

Chapter 7

BUYS IN THE 'HOOD

Bust out of that big box.

True or false?

- For every head of lettuce the United States exports to Mexico, it imports one head of lettuce from . . . Mexico.
- Britain imports—and exports—15,000 tons of waffles a year.
- Tomatoes are grown in California, shipped north to Canada for processing, and then shipped back to California as ketchup.

rue. True. And true.

All these pointless food swaps might be funny, if they didn't do so much harm. When we sit down to eat, our food has typically traveled about 1,500 miles to our plates. Think of all the fuel those ships and trucks burn up, and all the carbon dioxide they spew out—twenty-eight pounds for every gallon burned. It also takes a lot of energy to keep food cold. And if it's flown in . . . well, a 747 jet burns one gallon of fuel every *second*. So, just how "organic" is that chilled asparagus from Argentina?

Of course, if you live in North America and you want durian (a fruit so stinky that, in Singapore, you're not allowed to take it on the subway) or scrambled ackee (a Jamaican dish also known as "vegetable brains"), you may not be able to get it from the farmer up the road. But in one year, the United States exported over two million tons of milk and close to two million tons of potatoes, along with 734,000 tons of bacon, pork, and ham. Meanwhile, it *imported* nearly five million tons of milk, three million tons of potatoes, and 540,000 tons of bacon, pork, and ham. Why on earth should ordinary groceries like these crisscross the globe?

Again: follow the money. It will lead you to a handful of huge multinational corporations, which have driven out or taken over smaller supermarket chains around the world.

Part of the problem is that giant supermarket chains do business on a giant scale. They don't buy stuff for just one store. They buy it for thousands of stores. So they order from a big supplier who can ship them tons of what they want, year round, and cheap. Then they sort it out in huge regional warehouses and truck it to your town.

One study looked into what would happen if a farmer near Atlanta, Georgia, wanted to sell lettuce to a Safeway supermarket in Atlanta. It turned out the lettuce had to travel all the way up to Maryland for inspection, and then back again. The trip burned fuel and added shipping costs. It didn't do the lettuce much good, either.

But not-so-fresh lettuce may be the least of our worries. Ever heard the saying, "Don't put all your eggs in one basket?" Well, counting on a few big companies to feed us may—

Splat.

Who Are the Farmers in Your Neighborhood?

To find the CSAs and farmers' markets nearest you:

LocalHarvest.org

FoodRoutes.org

EatWellGuide.org

USDA Farmers Market Search (apps.ams.usda.gov/FarmersMarkets)

Oops. There go all our eggs.

The "splat" could be a drought, an early freeze, or a pest that gobbles up the crop. It could be a sudden rise in oil prices, making it expensive to ship food all over the globe. It could be a deadly virus passed from cow to cow on an enormous feedlot, mixed in with vast amounts of other meat in a centralized packing plant, and spread across the country by long-distance trucks.

Happily, there's another kind of food. Healthy. Fresh. Delicious. Planet-friendly. And you'll find it right around the corner. It's locally grown.

Every day, more people pass by supermarkets on their way to shop for local food. In 2008, the USDA reported 4,685 thriving farmers' markets, nearly twice as many as a dozen years before. Thousands of families signed up for shares in CSAs, "community supported agriculture." Members of CSAs pay the farmer ahead for the whole season.

Then, every week, they get a bag or box loaded with just-picked fruits and vegetables. Some CSAs offer other things, too—meat, eggs, milk, even fresh-cut flowers.

Locally grown food is popping up all over, from fancy four-star restaurants to burger joints. (Hey, you don't need to be a French chef to enjoy tomatoes that don't taste like Styrofoam.) Even school cafeterias are getting in on the act, hooking up with nearby farms to bring kids lunches that—*gasp*—don't come out of a freezer.

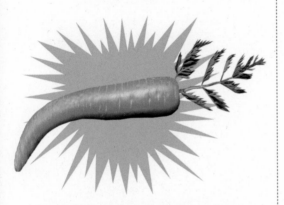

REBELS WITH A CAUSE

Squishy, tasteless carrots? Slimy green beans from a can? Not at Martin Luther King, Jr. Middle School in Berkeley, California. Thanks to the Edible Schoolyard program, students grow their own organic fruits and veggies and whip them up into school lunches that earn rave reviews. How much more local can you get?

But the Buy Local movement isn't only about food. It's about—well, everything!

Getting a decent bike from someone who will show you how to keep it in good shape, instead of heading to the Big-'n'-Cheap store for one that can't wait to fall apart. Hanging out at a local coffee shop that's funky and unique, not oozing with mass-produced trendiness. Browsing in a real bookstore, not the kind with a bored clerk who's never heard of anything for kids but *Harry Potter*.

Ditching the ugly suburban wasteland of the "big box" stores may be a no-brainer. But shifting your dollars to a local business brings more benefits than you might guess. For instance:

Honest prices . . .

Huh? Shopping at Wal-Mart may not be fun, but it *is* the cheapest place in town. Right?

Maybe not.

Curious about that slogan of "Always low prices," a team of researchers decided to find out if it was true. They went to stores in sixty cities and compared the prices on 3,800 items. On more than four items out of five, Wal-Mart *didn't* have the lowest price.

Chain stores have sneaky ways of making people think prices are low. For instance, they charge less for things we buy a lot, like milk and light bulbs. Shoppers know how much those things normally cost. So when they see a gallon of milk for a dollar, they think, "Wow! This store is cheap!" What they don't realize is that other items in their cart have been marked way, way up.

NO WAY!

Think you're getting a good deal? It may have nothing to do with the price tag. Research shows that shoppers connect bright lights and the color orange with very low prices. And you thought those store designers were just fashion challenged.

Even when you really do pay less, you may not get what you expect. Along with using sweatshops and "externalizing" costs (see chapters 3 and 5), chain stores can lower prices by selling stuff that looks good but is poorly made—in other words, cheap junk. (Ever have your backpack zipper break on the first day of school?)

Check out the prices at a local bike shop, music store, or clothes boutique. You may be surprised. Many independents have joined up in buying co-ops to get discounts like the chains—and pass the savings on to you.

goods, buy ads in local papers, and hire local people for everything from plumbing to Web site design. And when you're raising money for your team or a class trip, they're much more likely to help out. (Without making you wear a stupid T-shirt and sing advertising jingles.)

. . . Plus cash back

Hear that giant sucking sound? It's those "big box" stores, vacuuming up your money into a long pipe that leads straight back to headquarters.

When you spend your money at a locally owned store, it stays in town. Owners of independent businesses sell locally made

Freedom of choice

Oh, those oldies. Always telling you what you can watch or listen to or read. Parents. Teachers. Chain stores—

Wait a minute. Chain stores?

Oh, yeah.

Movie fans and music lovers have complained for years about Wal-Mart's refusal to sell anything it finds offensive—such as songs that criticize the store. Search their Web site for the latest album to download, and you're likely to see "edited" next to the title. Sounds so much nicer than "censored," doesn't it?

Then there are books. When you walk into a superstore, you see a lot of books. Probably way more books than your locally owned shop. (Unless you're lucky enough to live near a legendary indie such as BookPeople in Austin, Powell's Books in Portland, Oregon, or the Tattered Cover in Denver.)

Here's what you don't see: the books that aren't there.

HOW LOW CAN THEY GO?

When people started buying local, the mega-corporations knew they had to do something. But what? They couldn't _be_ local. So they'd just have to change the meaning of the word. Soon, Frito-Lay was airing ads for "local" chips. (Hey, those potatoes have to come from _somewhere_.) In Seattle, Starbucks pulled its sign off shops and gave them local-sounding names like "15th Avenue Coffee and Tea." And Barnes & Noble—where central buyers pick the books for stores across the country—tagged book recommendations on its website with the line "All bookselling is local." George Orwell would be proud.

Every independent bookstore decides for itself which books to carry. Chains, on the other hand, decide for all their stores. So even though they seem to offer lots of choice, it's the _same_ choice everywhere.

Long before a book comes out, the chain buyers get to put in their opinion. If they don't like the book, it may never be published. Sometimes publishers even turn down a book because they _think_ the chains won't like it.

Independent bookstores have a different kind of power—"handselling." That means they read the book, they love it, and they tell their customers about it. Face to face. One at a time.

It may not sound like much. But word of mouth is where all those "surprise" bestsellers come from. Ask Stephenie Meyer, whose _Twilight_ series got an early boost from Changing Hands Bookstore in Tempe, Arizona—Meyer's hometown. As she puts it, "Every writer needs an independent bookstore for a friend."

After-school jobs that don't start with "Mc"

Any kids you know work at a fast food place? How do they like their "careers"?

Probably not so much, writes Eric Schlosser in _Fast Food Nation_. He points out that two-thirds of fast-food robberies are inside jobs. That means the robber is (or was) a crew member—or even the manager!

Of course, most people who hate their

McJobs don't pull a ski mask on and grab a gun. They just quit . . . or goof around till they get fired. The average fast-food worker only lasts three or four months.

It's not just fast food. All kinds of chains offer crummy jobs with low pay. And they work hard to keep it that way: rubbing hours off employees' time sheets, bullying them if they try to join a union, and spending millions to fight off a few cents' raise in the minimum wage.

Local stores, on the other hand, often fight *for* a higher minimum wage. Why? Because they're already paying more. And they don't think it's fair for the big chains to weasel out of doing the right thing.

That nice warm fuzzy feeling . . . of not getting ripped off, dissed, and dumped

---

Did you know we're actually *paying* big box stores to take over our towns?

It's true! State and local governments roll out the red carpet for the chains, handing them millions of dollars to help build their stores. Why? Jobs and taxes. Bribe a giant company to set up shop, the politicians figure, and pretty soon the big bucks will start rolling in.

But that's not what happens.

Sure, the new store hires lots of people. But other people lose their jobs—better-paying jobs at the dozens of local stores the big box drives out of business. Chain stores slither out of paying taxes, too, thanks to a

tax dodge called the "Geoffrey Loophole" (after the Toys"R"Us mascot, Geoffrey the Giraffe).

To build their superstores, they bulldoze two-hundred-year-old landmarks. They chop down forests. They pave over farmland. They pollute the local water with illegal runoff from construction sites. They ruin neighborhoods and force people out of their homes.

And then, a few years later, they move out and build an even bigger store, leaving behind a giant, ugly, empty box.

FAST FORWARD

Communities around the country are getting creative with abandoned big box stores, turning them into schools, libraries, churches, flea markets, and fitness centers. In Texas, an old Wal-Mart was transformed into an indoor racetrack. And in Minnesota, a Kmart became The Spam Museum.

But people are saying, "Enough!" In towns across the United States and Canada, local groups have gathered to fight back—holding meetings, writing letters to the editor, signing petitions to keep out a superstore and save their town.

In her book *Big-Box Swindle*, Stacy Mitchell tells the story of a group in Charlevoix, Wisconsin, called This Is Our Town. The campaign really took off when a group of high school students got involved. "All of a sudden all the high school students were wearing buttons and talking to their parents about Wal-Mart," an organizer said. Popular opinion shifted, and the town drove Wal-Mart out.

According to sprawl-busters.com, nearly four hundred big box stores have been shot down by groups from Anchorage, Alaska to Zionsville, Indiana. Even better, the groups are pushing for new rules that limit sprawl, sew up the Geoffrey Loophole, and give local business a fair chance.

In Austin, Texas, a couple started a new fad when they passed out free bumper stickers urging locals to "Keep Austin Weird." In Bellingham, Washington, a team promoted local farms by entering the Ski to Sea race dressed up as a skiing carrot, a bicycling eggplant, and two peas in a canoe. And in Ithaca, New York, people use brightly colored paper money called "Ithaca hours" to pay for anything from an astrology reading to an ambulance ride.

A common slogan is "Think Local First." But why just first? If buying local is so great, then why buy *anything* that comes from far away?

Well, for one thing . . . we would sure miss chocolate.

MORE

- What's wrong with shopping at the chains? Big Box Mart (sendables.jibjab.com/originals/big_box_mart) sums it up in under two and a half minutes. This musical cartoon will leave you laughing, humming, and buying local.
- If you're green with envy over cafeterias with fresh sugar snap peas, Farmtoschool.org will help you get some local produce into your school lunch.
- Attention, activists! Whether you're fighting sprawl in your community or organizing a Buy Local Day, Bigboxtoolkit.com is your one-stop source.

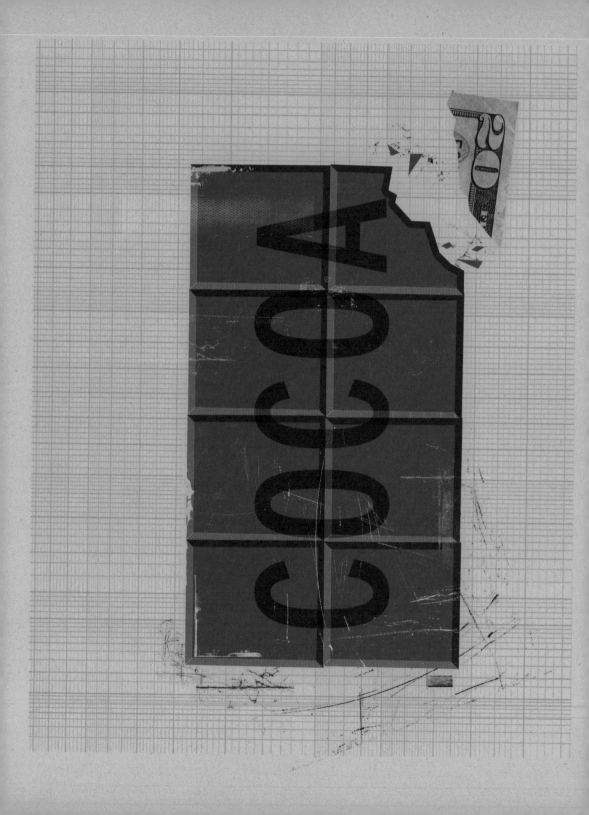

SWEETER TREATS

Wake up and smell the fair trade cocoa.

Before you finish eating breakfast in the morning, you've depended on more than half the world.

Martin Luther King, Jr. said that way back in 1967, but it's truer now than ever. Think: What did you have for breakfast? Maybe you poured a bowl of cereal, sweetened with sugar grown in Thailand, Costa Rica, or Malawi. Maybe you sipped a mug of cocoa from Bolivia or Ghana, while your mom or dad drank Nicaraguan, Ethiopian, or Indonesian coffee. Maybe you were in a hurry, so you just grabbed a banana from Jamaica or the Philippines. Or maybe you guzzled down chocolate, coffee,

sugar, *and* bananas. (Frozen banana mocha cappuccino, anyone?)

We depend on people all around the world for our breakfasts, and much more. That should be good news: They grow or make the stuff. We buy it. Everybody's happy. Right?

But in real life, it's not so simple. Between us stretches the "supply chain"—buyers, processors, and sellers who move products from a tropical plantation to our plate. A typical supply chain has eighteen links! And these middlemen (or middle *companies*—giant name brands like Dole and Nestlé dominate the chain) suck up most of the profits.

To get a rough idea, picture this:

You're sitting at the back of a school bus, your stomach grumbling. Luckily, your friend up at the front has a cranberry orange muffin to pass back to you. But wait! What's happening? Each kid is taking a big bite before handing the muffin on. It gets smaller and smaller. By the time it reaches you, there's nothing left but crumbs.

Now, nobody on the supply chain takes a bite of your banana or a gulp of cocoa. But they do take a bite out of your cash as it makes its way back to the farmer. A big bite. Lots of big, chomping, finger-lickin' bites.

When you pay a dollar for a chocolate bar, the cocoa farmer doesn't even get four cents. Bananas? Out of the supermarket price, producers snag a measly 5 percent. (And hired workers on plantations are paid hardly anything.)

The makers of the movie *Black Gold* filmed a group of African coffee farmers reacting to the news that in America, coffee drinkers often paid as much as $2.90 a cup. The farmers couldn't believe it. At the prices they were getting for their coffee beans, they would have to sell at least twenty kilos—enough to brew *1600 cups* of coffee—before they earned $2.90.

One farmer imagined how he would feel if the price went up to fifty-seven cents a kilo—less than a penny a cup. "We would soar high above the sky," he said. That price "would change our lives beyond recognition."

So why don't they raise their prices?

Let's say you come from a family of coffee farmers. You've worked hard growing your coffee beans, and now you and your dad are taking them to sell. With the money, he'll buy rice to feed your family. Maybe he'll even buy you a pair of shoes, so you can walk the seven miles to the nearest school.

The buyer weighs your beans and calls a number out. The weight sounds low. You and your dad are pretty sure he's cheating you, but what can you do? He's the one with the scale. Then you hear the price, and your heart sinks. It's even less than what he paid last time. When your dad protests, the buyer shrugs and says, "World prices have gone down."

Maybe he's telling the truth. Maybe he's not. There's no way to be sure, because he is the only buyer who comes to your village.

You could take your coffee to a bigger town—if you had any way to get it there. You could switch over to a better-paying crop—if you had money to buy seeds and tools, and if your worn-out patch of land would grow anything else.

Instead, you swallow hard as your dad takes the small handful of coins, and months of grueling work vanish up the supply chain into someone else's pockets. Someone like the CEO of Starbucks, who earned nearly $10 million in 2008.

It isn't fair.

But penniless farmers all over the world are banding together to break the chain. They've formed associations, unions, and cooperatives. They've chipped in to buy their own scales, and chosen somebody they know and trust to do the weighing. And when they sell their products, they look for a special kind of buyer: one committed to fair trade.

What's so fair about fair trade? Partly, of course, the pay. Under fair trade, farmers are guaranteed a decent price that they can count on not to drop all of a sudden. They're also paid ahead of time, so they don't have to borrow money (at a sky-high rate of interest) just to plant their season's crops.

ACT OUT!

People pay attention when you give them chocolate. That's the idea behind "reverse trick-or-treating"—going door to door on Halloween and handing out samples of fair trade chocolate, along with a card explaining all about fair trade. Order your free kit (chocolate included) from www. ReverseTrickorTreating.org.

Fair trade also pays a "social premium." This doesn't go to each separate farmer, but to the whole community. Together, they decide how to use it to improve their lives. They might buy a tractor, or start building a new school. Or they might dig a village well so that girls don't have to keep hauling heavy buckets of water home from a polluted river miles away.

But there's more to fair trade than money. Fair trade groups encourage farmers to protect the planet and their families by cutting out dangerous chemical pesticides and fertilizers—then help them do the paperwork for the organic seal. On bigger plantations, fair trade requires safe and healthy work conditions and a living wage for hired laborers. (And, duh . . . no kidnapped child slaves.)

Most important, many fair trade groups work hard to change the rules that make world trade so *un*fair. For instance, they push to end subsidies. Thanks to these extra payments, big growers in the United States and Europe can afford to "dump" their goods at a very low price in poor countries. Then the local farmers, who don't get free money from their own government, can't sell their cotton or cocoa for a fair price at home. Meanwhile, rich countries place high import taxes on processed goods such as jeans and chocolate bars (taxes that are *higher* for goods from the poorest countries). That drives local factories out of business, leaving the farmers just one choice: to sell their raw materials to powerful multinational companies at a low price.

"Free trade agreements" are a major problem, too. The word *free* makes them sound nice. Who doesn't want more freedom? But in reality, these deals only make huge corporations free. Free to go into poor countries and suck up all their natural resources. Free to hire workers at low wages and then drive them till they drop. Free to leave behind a terrible environmental mess. The local people, and their governments, are *less* free. They can't even pass laws to protect themselves and their environment—that would get in the way of "free" trade.

Some people say that's just the way it is. But the growth of fair trade proves there is another way. And the more shoppers switch over to fair trade, the more people it helps. Already, fair trade businesses have changed the lives of more than five million producers and their families.

HOW LOW CAN THEY GO?

Fair trade chocolate and bananas cost more, but is all that money going to poor farmers? British researchers caught supermarket chains charging higher markups on fair trade items. So they were buying them for a little more, but selling them for a lot more—and keeping the extra cash.

Asked about fair trade, thirteen-year-old Raphael Agyapong said enthusiastically, "Fair trade has helped me a lot and a lot!" Raphael's family belongs to Kuapa Kokoo, a cocoa farmers' union in Ghana. Their motto is "Pa Pa Paa," which means "the best of the best of the best."

Kuapa Kokoo teamed up with a fair trade group, Twin Trading, to create a company called Divine Chocolate. The farmers don't just sell their cocoa to Divine—they own nearly half the company. So, instead of tiny crumbs of the chocolate dollar, they receive a nice big chunk.

Working with Comic Relief (a famous British charity started by comedians), Divine launched Dubble, the first fair trade chocolate bar for kids. The Dubble Web site urges kids to join up as "Dubble agents" and use "positive pester power" to get stores to "stock the choc." Visitors to the site can also sign the Chocolate Challenge Manifesto, aimed at making the entire chocolate industry switch over to fair trade.

With a little digging, you can find all kinds of things fair trade, from soccer balls to sneakers to shampoo. But how can you be sure the folks who make this stuff really are getting a fair deal? One way is to look for a label showing that the product is certified by a fair trade group. (In North America, it's TransFair Canada or TransFair USA.) Or a company or store may display the seal of the Fair Trade Federation or the World Fair Trade Organization, meaning that *all* the goods it sells are fair trade.

Online, many fair trade companies post photos of people who make the products, along with their stories. The Web site of the Thanksgiving Coffee Company, for instance, explains how its coffee comes from Jewish, Muslim, and Christian farmers in Uganda, who formed a co-op called Mirembe Kawomera, or "Delicious Peace." And at Fairtradeproof.org, customers can type in the lot number from a bag of coffee beans and see the actual paperwork signed by farmers, showing what they have been paid.

But fair trade can go even farther.

Imagine a dark, moonless night, deep in the forests of Brazil. A creaky pickup truck bumps up a dirt trail to a mountaintop. Several men jump out. They look around. Then one of them pulls out . . . a laptop?

The mountain gets the strongest signal. That's why they've come up here late at night, when wireless rates are lowest. They're uploading a new online store to sell their co-op's hand-embroidered clothes.

Using a program called OpenEntry, artisans around the world can cut out the middleman completely. The free software lets them set up a Web site, sell directly to customers, and keep every penny for themselves. OpenEntry is designed to make it easy for people without a lot of computer skills to handle tasks like creating a catalog and taking payments by credit card.

These people may live in places that don't even have paved roads or electricity. But thanks to satellites and solar cells, they can skip over what they've missed and jump straight into the twenty-first century. That's known as "leapfrogging."

Cool, huh?

If high-tech solutions make you happy, hang on to your hard drive. 'Cause you ain't seen nothing yet. . . .

MORE

- To get the buzz on coffee, don't ask that chipper barista with the high-caf smile. The movie *Black Gold* reveals what's really going on.
- Want to get to know a cocoa farmer's kid? Equal Exchange can hook you up. Sign up for a pen pal at equalexchange.coop/fair-trade-fundraiser-program-pen-pals.
- You may not be old enough to vote, but it's never too soon to fight for justice. Check out United Students for Fair Trade (usft.org) or the Student Trade Justice Campaign (tradejusticecampaign.org).

MAKIN' IT

Try on these designer greens.

Some people in the world need more stuff, like water, food, a pair of shoes, a phone. Some people need less stuff, like bottled water, junk food, *piles* of shoes, *another* phone. But one thing everybody needs right now is BETTER stuff.

Imagine . . .

- Takeout containers you can toss right on the ground—where they turn into fertilizer for the flower seeds hidden inside.
- Jeans dyed in a factory where water goes in clean and comes out . . . cleaner!
- A school that's wired to let the lights and computers draw their power from feet pounding down the hallway between classes.

These aren't pie-in-the-sky fantasies. We can do it. We have the technology—thanks to green design.

Green design (aka eco, or sustainable, design) simply means trying to make things without hurting anyone or making a mess of the planet. In green design, you don't just ask, "How can we make this so it's a little less bad?" Instead, you ask, "How can we make this so it's good?"

Take shampoo. You can make it not so bad by pulling *out* a harmful chemical ("paraben-free"). To make it good, you have to start from scratch, and only put *in* those ingredients that had been proven safe.

Or paper. Buy recycled printer paper, and fewer trees get chopped down. Definitely not so bad. But what if paper wasn't made of trees at all? What if it came from a fast-growing plant like hemp or the West African *kenaf*?

What makes most recycling "not as bad" instead of "good" is that too often, recycling is really *down*cycling. Plastic, for instance, loses quality when it's recycled. You can turn a plastic yogurt tub into a toothbrush, and the toothbrush into plastic lumber for a playground. And that's fine. It means less waste, less oil burned, and less pollution. But sooner or later, that plastic will still end up in the same place—the dump.

CHANGE THE GAME

The bottles and newspapers you toss in the recycling bin may end up at the landfill sooner than you think. Recycling depends on someone *buying* those materials to recycle. If it's easier and cheaper to use raw materials, then no one buys the stuff, and it goes to the dump. The fix? Charging a fair price for raw materials, instead of giving our natural resources away free. Legally requiring all manufactured items to contain a certain percentage of recycled materials. And takeback laws work, too. Once tire makers had to take old tires back, they found all kinds of ways to use the rubber, from mouse pads to sneaker soles.

Recycling is a good start. But green designers say it's not enough to slow stuff down on its way to the dump. We need to design it better in the first place, so that it stays useful (in some form) forever. That's the idea of "zero waste."

But how can zero waste be possible? Won't we always have to throw things out?

We do throw out a lot. In fact, 80 percent of what we buy is meant to be used just once. (Think candy wrapper, soda bottle, plastic straw . . .) But the weird thing is, this throwaway stuff is designed as if we wanted it to last forever.

Here's what we do: Take oil that has been around since the time of the dinosaurs. Turn it into plastic. Wrap it around a snack that sits on a shelf a few weeks and then is eaten in five minutes. Drop it in a landfill for the next five hundred years.

Does that make any sense at all?

POWER TO THE PEOPLE

Seeing those flimsy plastic bags blowing across roads, hanging from branches, and floating in rivers, South Africans used to jokingly call them the "national flower." Now they're gone, thanks to a growing world movement to save oil, reduce pollution, and prevent harm to marine life by banning the bag. Cities from New Delhi to Los Angeles have jumped on board. China outlawed the "white pollution" in 2008—a move that could save thirty-seven million barrels of oil a year.

If you go to the yearly Green Festival in Seattle, San Francisco, Denver, Chicago, or Washington, D.C., you'll see crowds of people chowing down on fresh organic food—served with plastic forks and knives.

A bunch of eco-phonies? No. The forks and knives are made out of potato starch. The plastic cups are made of corn. The paper plates are made from sugarcane. And all of it goes straight into the compost bin.

Bio-plastics use ingredients that grow in months, instead of millions of years. They take less energy to make, and create less pollution. Unlike plastics made from oil, they don't have nasty chemicals you may be swallowing. And once they're composted, they feed the soil, helping new plants grow.

Of course, they only compost if you *put* them in the compost. Buried in a landfill, bio-plastic may not break down any quicker than regular plastic. (Though at least it isn't adding toxins to the water, soil, and air.)

That's why the shoe company Brooks started designing sneakers for the dump. That doesn't mean they're junky. They won't fall apart on your feet or in your closet—unless your closet happens to be airless, damp, and teeming with microbes, like a landfill. (Hmm . . . maybe it's time to clean?) But in the landfill, they'll break down in twenty years. Sounds like a long time? Well, ordinary shoes may last up to a *thousand* years.

Here's the coolest part: the folks at Brooks decided not to patent their invention. So other sneaker companies can copy them, for free.

If we want to send our stuff back to nature, we need to make sure it belongs there. No chemicals that make us sick. Nothing that turns cute little tadpoles into mutant freaks. Nothing you wouldn't want to swim in, breathe, or eat.

Now, a lot of stuff is just plain bad and shouldn't be used to make anything at all. But everything can't be made out of garden vegetables. What about the things that need high-tech ingredients, like cell phones and TVs?

Not a problem, say green designers William McDonough and Michael Braungart. They've helped green all kinds of products, from surf wax that doesn't trash the beach to eco-friendly body wash in recycled plastic bottles signed by movie star Brad Pitt.

Their book *Cradle to Cradle: Remaking the Way We Make Things* splits materials into two types: the type we can compost and the type we can recycle. The key is not to mix them up. That way, what will be recycled stays high-quality, and what will be returned to the earth stays clean and safe.

Cradle to Cradle isn't made of paper. Instead, it's printed on plastic pages with a special nontoxic ink. Return it to the factory, the authors say, and the ink can be scrubbed off and reused, while the plastic can be used over and over without down-cycling to the dump.

But how can we be sure a plastic book—or phone, or anything else—will make it back to the factory for recycling? After all, once it goes out the door, it doesn't belong to the company that made it anymore. It's yours. And when it breaks, wears out, or simply isn't useful anymore, well . . . it's still yours.

But what if it wasn't? What if companies had to take back whatever they made? Probably, they'd be a lot more careful about what they put in their products (such as hazardous chemicals), and they'd design them to be easily recycled. After all, if you ran a factory, which would you rather get back: valuable materials, or toxic junk?

ACT OUT!

Annoyed because something you bought can't be recycled? Green America (greenamericatoday.org) says, send it back! Mail it to the manufacturers, along with a note asking them to close the loop.

It makes sense for consumers, too. If you think about it, buying a TV or phone isn't like buying a slice of pizza. With the pizza, what you're paying for is what it's made of—cheese and sauce and crust. But do you *want* each of the 4,360 chemicals in your TV? Or do you just want to be able to flip on your favorite show?

We're not really paying for the *thing*. We're paying for what it does for us. So instead of companies selling us a fridge, say, maybe they should just sell us what we want—a way to keep food fresh. The fridge would still be humming away in the kitchen. But when it wore out, the company would deliver a new model, and take the old one back to the factory for recycling.

(Green designers have some fancy names for this idea, like "products of service," "extended producer responsibility," and "the functional economy." You could also call it "renting." But whatever.)

Still, the product itself is a small part of the story. Remember, if you add up all the stuff it takes to make it and get it to the store, what you see on the shelf is only 5 percent! What about everything that was torn up, chopped down, flushed out, burned, or trashed along the way?

NO WAY!

Canada's boreal forest is one of the last great ancient forests on the planet—and it's being chopped down to make *toilet paper*. Find out more at kleercut.net.

To get to zero waste, we need to change the process from a line into a loop. In a line, you start with a big heap of raw materials and end with a big heap of . . . garbage. In a loop, there's no such thing as garbage. Anything a factory spits out is picked up and used somewhere else. Fabric scraps turn into felt or garden mulch. Ash goes in cement. Steam is piped to nearby homes for heat or to another factory to power its machines.

If this sounds only natural, that's because it is. In nature, nothing's ever wasted. Everything is food for somebody. Carpenter ants eat fallen trees. Vultures eat carrion. And dung beetles—well, you know.

Deforestation, Boreal Forest.
Image © Ian Graham/iStock

More and more, designers are looking to nature to find out what works. After all, if it's in nature, it has already been tested for a long, long time! This approach is known as biomimicry. (In Europe, it's got a niftier name: bionics.)

You may not have heard of biomimicry before, but you've seen and touched it—at least, if you've ever used Velcro. The guy who invented it came up with the idea after taking his dog for a walk. Seeing the way burrs stuck to the dog's fur, he wondered if he could make a new fastener that used a similar design.

Today, biomimics are eyeing other natural wonders, such as the banana spider. This web-slinger spins a thread that, ounce for ounce, is many times stronger than steel or even Kevlar (used to make bullet-proof vests). It's also stretchier than any bungee cord. Some of that Spidey power could be pretty useful in a tennis racket or a parachute.

Then there's the gecko, a lizard whose toes stick to anything, even underwater—then peel off without a trace. Could "gecko tape" let people walk on walls and ceilings? Maybe. But it also could be used in place of glues and solvents that leave toxic residues, making the things we use safer to compost or easier to recycle.

Biomimicry isn't just about *what* nature makes, but *how*. If you go in a factory, you'll probably see lots of DANGER signs. Everywhere you look, there's something that could burn you or explode or eat right through your skin. Nature tends to be a little more laid back. Think of a firefly. Its rear end is a nifty gadget that lights up without getting hot, just like the LED lights on your microwave or phone. But while the chips for LEDs are made in super-hot high pressure chambers, fireflies are made in places you might actually enjoy hanging out—say, a nice patch of leafy woods beside a running stream.

And where does nature get the fuel it needs to manufacture fireflies, and sticky gecko feet, and all the rest? Hint: It's a clean, safe, non-polluting energy source. And it isn't running out.

It's sunlight. And every forty minutes, enough hits the earth to power all the cars, planes, houses, factories, schools, roller coasters, iPods, electric guitars, and everything else on the planet that needs energy—for a whole *year*.

Catching some rays is getting easier and easier. Using "Power Plastic," a Massachusetts company called Konarka says it can print solar cells on anything from backpacks to remote-controlled toy cars. Meanwhile, in California, Cool Earth Solar has come up with a shiny silver "solar balloon" that's cheap, easy to make, and puts out four hundred times the power of an ordinary solar cell.

Sun, wind, raindrops, ocean waves—if it moves, it can be used for electricity. One scientist in Ontario, Canada, has even invented a "vortex engine" that makes energy by whipping up its own tornadoes.

REBELS WITH A CAUSE

Some say that North Dakota's wind power could take the place of Saudi Arabian oil. But how to get the message out? To three extreme-sports-loving guys named Jason, Sam, and Paul, the answer was obvious: snow-kites! In winter 2008, the 2XtM team kite-skied across the state, braving frostbite, barbed-wire fences, and wild gusts. *Whoosh!*

Then there's good old people power. At the Sustainable Dance Club in the Netherlands, the dancing feet light up the floor. And a Hong Kong gym rigged up its exercise machines to run the TV sets.

People power isn't only for the rich and trendy. In 2008, a team of students won Google's "Innovate or Die" contest with their tricycle that filters water while you pedal. Say you live in a village without running water. You bike down to the river, fill the tank, and by the time you pedal home, the water's sparkling clean and safe to drink.

To make something that's really eco-friendly, you have to answer lots of questions. What's in it? Are the materials safe? Where did they come from? (An endangered forest? An open-pit mine?) How is the product made? Who makes it? Are they treated fairly? Will it take a lot of energy to make? To run? Where is that energy going to come from? How can it be made without pollution or waste? And when it reaches the end of its life, where will it go?

It's exciting. But it isn't easy.

Some folks are psyched to meet the challenge. Tom Szaky and Jon Beyer were still in their teens when they got the idea to make plant food out of garbage, and package it in recycled plastic bottles. Today, their company, TerraCycle, also turns old newspapers into pencils, Oreo cookie wrappers into notebook covers, and juice pouches into backpacks.

On the other hand, some folks are not so psyched. They'd rather spend their time and energy on something else. Like faking it.

MORE

- How do whales teach us about wind power? How does a tree show us the way to build a stronger, lighter car? Click on *Case studies* at biomimicryinstitute.org, and as the tagline says, "Prepare to be inspired."

- Quit thinking about the same old boring stuff. If it's new, smart, and sustainable, you'll find it at world-changing.com.

Chapter 10

GREEN WARRIORS VS. GREENWASHERS

How to tell the heroes from the zeros.

Lately, it seems like every company is trying hard to turn itself around. Dunkin' Donuts offers fair trade lattes. Coca-Cola helps set up a research center to develop eco-packaging. Nike promises to be completely "climate neutral" by 2011.

The name of the game is CSR, or corporate social responsibility. The rules? Companies need to become better citizens. Instead of looking only at the bottom line—how much money they can make—CSR says businesses must have a triple bottom line: people, planet, *and* profits.

Can businesses do well by doing good? Ask outdoor clothing maker Patagonia, one of the greenest companies around. Since 1993, they've kept millions of plastic soda bottles out of landfills by turning them into warm, soft fleece. All their cotton is organic. They recycle worn-out clothes, even from other companies. And, with a Web site feature called The Footprint Chronicles, they let customers click on a picture of a product and follow it from design to delivery, seeing its impact—good and bad—along the way.

Picture yourself at the supermarket or the mall. You scan a bar code with your phone, it runs a speedy online search, and everything you want to know about the product and the company shows up on the little screen. Reality? Not yet. But any minute now . . .

Then there's Clif Bar & Company. Buy one of their organic Clif Kids snacks or energy bars, and they'll pay you to return the wrapper to TerraCycle for "upcycling" into a backpack. They run their trucks on biodiesel, hand out gift cards as rewards for walking, biking, or carpooling to work, and pay employees to take the day off and volunteer.

Patagonia and Clif Bar both belong to 1% for the Planet, a group of businesses that pledge to donate 1 percent of their profits to help save the environment. But they have something else in common, too. They're both privately owned.

What does that mean, and why does it matter?

Suppose you call up Clif Bar and ask,

"Who's in charge?" The answer will be, "Gary and Kit."

Gary Erickson and Kit Crawford own the company. They don't answer to anybody else. So, if they want to buy a bunch of bicycles and let workers take a spin on their lunch break, they can. If they'd like to let the local CSA leave veggies in their fridge for pickup, they go right ahead. And if they decide to help employees switch to hybrid cars by chipping in company money—well, it ain't nobody's business if they do.

Ben & Jerry's used to be a privately owned company. So did The Body Shop, and Tom's of Maine. All three were famous for taking care of people and the environment. Then Ben & Jerry's sold out to the food giant Unilever. The Body Shop went to L'Oréal. And Tom's of Maine became part of Colgate-Palmolive.

The new owners promised to uphold the same ideals. But was that possible?

The difference between a huge multinational corporation and a company like Patagonia or Clif Bar isn't just the size. It isn't even the values of the people who run it. The real difference is what a public corporation *is*.

A public library belongs to all the people. So does a public park or swimming pool. A public company, on the other hand, isn't actually public at all. It belongs to its shareholders.

When a company "goes public," it sells chunks of itself on the stock market. These chunks are known as shares. The investors who buy shares are called shareholders. As a group, the shareholders now own the company.

Legally, a corporation is set up to do one thing: make money for its shareholders. The CEO is not allowed to put anything else ahead of profits. Not making a safe product. Not trying to pollute less. Not paying workers enough to live on. Nothing.

Massive layoffs. Sweatshops. Killer chemicals. Pollution. Toxic waste. Deforestation. Global warming. If it earns or saves them money, it makes sense to do.

The folks who run a corporation may be perfectly nice people. But, as the film *The Corporation* argues, the corporation itself is a psychopath. It's designed to be selfish. It has no sense of right and wrong. It will lie, cheat, steal, and even kill to make a profit. And it's totally unable to feel guilt.

POWER TO THE PEOPLE

After an eleven-year-old boy died from riding his bike over toxic sludge, some towns in Pennsylvania tried to get the corporations that spread sludge to pay for safety tests. That's when they found out that, under U.S. law, a corporation is a "person"— a super-rich, super-powerful person that can launch a zillion-dollar lawsuit any time small-town officials do something it doesn't like.

Something stank, and it wasn't only the sludge. So the real live people of Porter Township, Pennsylvania passed the nation's first Corporate Personhood Elimination ordinance. It simply said that, in their town, a company was NOT a human being.

So, can corporations ever be "socially responsible"?

Only if it helps them make a profit.

That's where we come in. After all, we're the ones who buy the stuff they sell. And if we tell them we're not buying any more till they shape up, they pay attention.

Protests by high school students and other anti-sweatshop activists have forced brands like Reebok and The Gap to be more open about how their clothes are made. Under pressure from consumers, Starbucks agreed to buy twice as much fair trade coffee in 2009. And after the environmental group ForestEthics ran its "Victoria's Dirty Secret" ads, which featured models in their undies holding chainsaws, the company pledged to start using recycled paper for its catalogues.

Corporations change their ways to save their reputation and their customers. They also change if they see a chance to sell something new. When people ask for fair trade chocolate, grass-fed burgers, or sweatshop-free clothes (or barf-flavored jelly beans, or *anything*), corporations jump to give them what they want.

Unless, of course, it's easier and cheaper just to fake it.

Faking it is also known as "greenwashing"—doing the same old thing, but with a thin layer of green on top. (*Green* as in "good for people and the planet.")

There are lots of ways a company can greenwash. It can spend a little on green programs . . . then spend a whole lot more broadcasting ads about those programs. It can make loud, attention-getting promises . . . then, once the hoopla has died down, quietly let them slide. It can make little changes, but fight laws that would force them to make bigger ones. It can donate money to environmental groups (and get a tax break), then go right on hacking down old forests and blowing up mountaintops.

Greenwashing can work on a whole company, or a specific product. In one study, researchers from TerraChoice Environmental Marketing went into half a dozen big box stores and picked out 1,018 items that made environmental claims. Out of all those items, guess how many they found that, in their opinion, *weren't* false or misleading?

One.

A few of these claims were outright fibs, like items claiming to be certified organic when they weren't. More commonly, they failed to offer proof, or the claims were too vague to really mean anything. ("All natu-

ral," for instance—arsenic is natural, but you don't want it in your peanut butter!)

The biggest problem was what the researchers called "the hidden trade-off." That's when we think a product's greener than it really is, because we're only told one thing about it. Recycled paper, for example, may be white and bright because it's made with toxic chlorine bleach. Electronics may be energy-efficient, but have lead inside which leaks out in the landfill.

Does that mean we shouldn't bother with recycled and energy-efficient products? No. But it does mean that if we want to get the big picture, it may be more helpful to use eco-labels such as EcoLogo and Green Seal, which look at a product's total impact over its whole "life," from raw materials to recycling. In the United Kingdom, the Carbon Trust adds up the carbon dioxide put out over the entire life cycle of a specific item such as a men's medium size black hoodie or a bag of organic potatoes, and marks the number on a cute little "carbon footprint" for the label.

*

Surprisingly, some companies are doing just the opposite of greenwashing. They're making changes quietly, behind closed doors. Why? One reason is that drawing attention to what they're doing right can also draw attention to what they're doing wrong. When Levi Strauss first started

GREEN WARRIORS
VS. GREENWASHERS

WHAT TO ASK?

What do you mean, you're green? Vague phrases like "good for the planet," "eco-friendly," "natural," and "environmentally safe" don't mean a whole lot. Look for details, either on the packaging or the company Web site.

Who says? Are their claims backed up by a third party? Are they certified? Learn what the different labels mean, and go with those you trust.

Are you serious? A company may talk a lot about its fair trade coffee or organic soap. But if those products are just a tiny percentage of their business, well . . . numbers don't lie.

What does Google say? Of course, you can't believe everything you read online. But if you type in a brand name, plus a word like *sweatshop*, *ethics*, or *environment*, you'll find out pretty fast if it's up to its eyeballs in bad mojo.

Do you think I'm stupid? Hey, don't be afraid to use your common sense! Claiming to be "free" of something that's illegal anyway, like CFCs, is just plain silly. So is boasting that a brand of juice has no trans fats. (Neither does any other juice!) And any company that tells you buying *anything* will "save the earth" is full of you-know-what.

WHERE TO GO?

Betterworldshopper.org
Consumer Reports Greener Choices
(greenerchoices.org)

The EnviroMedia
Greenwashing Index
(greenwashingindex.com)

buying 2 percent organic cotton, they didn't trumpet the news. Talking about the terrible effects of cotton pesticides, they feared, would only make customers ask, "What about the other 98 percent?"

When huge corporations say they're going green, it's hard to know what to think. Is it a real turnaround, or just a slick new ad campaign? Should we encourage them by shopping there, or stick to local stores and companies that have been greener all along? Are some corporations too bad to be good?

Case in point: Wal-Mart. When the mega-store announced a slew of changes—cutting energy use, trimming packaging, selling organic food at the "Wal-Mart price"—some activists cheered. Wal-Mart is so big and powerful, they pointed out, that any move it makes is a shot heard 'round the world. If Wal-Mart set serious standards for suppliers, the race to the bottom could spin on its heel and zoom straight up to the top.

Others argued that even a "greener" Wal-Mart would still cause enormous harm. It wouldn't stop shipping products all around the world, or pushing factories to sell them stuff so cheap that workers couldn't possibly be paid a decent wage. It would still be paving over fields with mammoth parking lots that poison our rivers with toxic runoff. Local businesses would still go under. Local people would continue growing poorer. Environmentalist Bill McKibben sums it

up: "There's something gross about buying a healthy carrot from a sick company."

Wal-Mart's choice to change may be phony baloney. Or it may be the real deal. But is that even the point?

Shouldn't we be asking, *Why is it a choice?*

Why does Brand X get to choose whether or not to sell jeans made in sweatshops? Who elected corporations to decide how much pollution should be in the air we breathe? When did we agree to put ourselves, our planet, and our future in the manicured hands of a bunch of multi-millionaires whose job is to look out for number one—their company—and no one else?

Corporations are not of the people, by the people, for the people. Government is. From local school boards and town councils right up to presidents and prime ministers, democratic governments exist to do what's best for *us*.

Now we need to make them get off their butts and do it.

We have to force our politicians to quit taking money from big corporations and letting them set the rules. We have to demand to know what's in the stuff we buy, where and how it is made, and what it's doing to our health and the health of the planet. We have to make companies pay their share of taxes so that *we* can decide how *our* money should be spent.

We need laws to make *all* companies do

the right thing for people and the earth. Together, we need to create a world in which everybody has a voice.

CHANGE THE GAME

Property laws give people—and companies—the right to own and use pieces of nature. But what if nature had its own rights? In Ecuador, it does. The country's new constitution guarantees nature "the right to exist, persist, maintain, and regenerate its vital cycles." Hmm . . . Twenty-eighth Amendment, anyone?

We need to take back our power.

It isn't a fair fight. Corporations are rich, powerful, and used to running things. But we, the people, have a secret weapon that can turn them into helpless blobs of Jell-O. It's a piece of paper handed out by the government, which allows a corporation to exist. It's called the corporate charter. And without it, the biggest, baddest, most out-of-control zillion-dollar corporation is nothing at all.

We, the people, can rip up that piece of paper. We can close companies down. And we can restore corporate charters to what they once were—not a right, but a privilege, granted only to companies that pledge to serve the common good.

Now *that's* social responsibility.

MORE

- Who's the slimiest of them all? Check out the latest "10 Worst Corporations" list at multi-nationalmonitor.org. Then surf over to opensecrets.org and see which politicians they've got in their pockets.
- Need a network? With members from Zimbabwe to Afghanistan, TakingITGlobal (tigweb.org) is "the largest online community of youth interested in global issues and creating positive change."

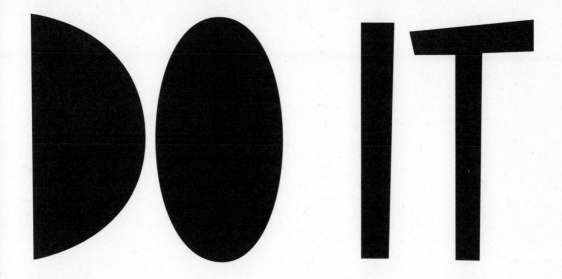

DO IT

Change starts now.

"The world is being destroyed—no doubt about it—by the greed of the rich and powerful. It is also being destroyed by popular demand. There are not enough rich and powerful people to consume the whole world; for that, the rich and powerful need the help of countless ordinary people."

—Wendell Berry

o, you ready to run out there and start buying lots and lots of the right stuff? Sweatshop-free, fair trade, organic, local, green—

Stop.

Go back to chapter 1.

Remember those unequal slices of blueberry pie? The seventy full garbage cans we never see? The THING that is devouring the world?

Yes, buying better is important. But if we want fresh air, clean water, and plenty of pie to go around, it's even more important to buy less.

It doesn't have to hurt. Start easy. Skip something you don't really want—say, bottled water. One plastic bottle may not seem like much. But it is actually huge. Think of those garbage cans. For every bottle you don't buy (or candy bar or pair of jeans or skateboard deck or game or phone or, hey, this book—get it out of the library!), multiply it times seventy. That's how much *stuff* you're saving from the dump.

The Center for a New American Dream printed a great little paper pouch that you can stick a credit card or money in.

Every **dollar** I spend is a **statement** about the kind of **world** I want & the **quality of life** I value.

new
american
dream

More fun, less stuff, & more of what matters

www.newdream.org • 1-877-68-DREAM
Printed on 100% recycled paper

Sample questions to ask before buying:
- Is this something I need?
- Do I already own something that could serve the same purpose?
- Can I borrow one, find one used, or make one instead of buying new?
- Was it made locally?
- Was it made with environmentally preferable materials?
- Was it made with fair labor practices?
- Will it serve more than one purpose?
- Will it be easy and cost-effective to maintain?
- Will using it require excessive energy?
- Does it come in excessive packaging?
- Can I recycle or compost it when I'm done with it?
- If I'm still not sure, can I wait a month before deciding to buy it?

For something small enough to slip into your wallet, it sure says a lot!

Not to go all Oprah on you now, but change isn't as hard as you might think. Here's how it works. One day, just for the fun of it, you do something a little different. Let's say you buy an organic cotton T-shirt. All of a sudden, *you're* a little different. You're the kind of person who spends a bit extra to buy an organic T-shirt.

Maybe the next afternoon you're thinking about hitting McDonald's for a burger. But something doesn't feel quite right. It isn't *you*. You care enough about pesticides on cotton to buy an organic shirt. So why would you swallow the whole factory farm mess? Not to mention what you know is in the meat.

One locally grown lunch.

One awesome thrift store find.

One fair trade birthday gift for your best friend.

Before you know it, you're totally hooked on buying less and buying better. But that's not all. You're asking questions in the stores. You're talking to your friends. You're writing to your senator. You're blogging. You're creating protest art. Maybe you're even putting on some street theater for Buy Nothing Day.

You're so freakin' famous, they beg you to be a contestant on that new TV show, *Real Deal.*

Lights. Camera. Action—

"Welcome!" The host beams. "Today, we have a real treat...."

You stare at the two chocolate bars.

The choice is obvious. You know exactly what to do.

You grab the bar labeled "organic" and "fair trade." You toss it to the hungry boy.

Then you march straight off the sound-stage, push past the blinding lights, and go find out who in the world is running this crazy show.

More!

To Read

Chew on This: Everything You Don't Want to Know about Fast Food by Eric Schlosser and Charles Wilson (Houghton Mifflin, 2006)

The Ear, the Eye and the Arm by Nancy Farmer (Orchard Books, 2004)

Feed by M. T. Anderson (Candlewick Press, 2002)

The Gospel According to Larry by Janet Tashjian (Henry Holt, 2001)

Made You Look: How Advertising Works and Why You Should Know by Shari Graydon and Warren Clark (Annick Press, 2003)

The Omnivore's Dilemma: The Secrets Behind What You Eat (Young Readers Edition) by Michael Pollan (Dial, 2009)

So Yesterday by Scott Westerfeld (Razorbill, 2004)

Stuff: The Secret Lives of Everyday Things by Alan Thein Durning and John C. Ryan (Northwest Environment Watch, 1997)

What the World Eats by Faith D'Aluisio and Peter Menzel (Tricycle Press, 2008)

To Watch

Black Gold directed by Marc Francis and Nick Francis (2006)

China Blue directed by Micha X. Peled (2006)

Frontline: The Merchants of Cool directed by Barak Goodman (PBS, 2001)

King Corn directed by Aaron Woolf (2007)

Maxed Out: Hard Times, Easy Credit and the Era of Predatory Lenders directed by James D. Scurlock (2006)

McLibel: The Story of Two People Who Wouldn't Say McSorry directed by Franny Armstrong (2005)

Wal-Mart: The High Cost of Low Price directed by Robert Greenwald (2005)

What Would Jesus Buy? directed by Rob VanAlkemade (2007)

Online

Behindthelabel.org

Betterworldshopper.org

Bigboxtoolkit.com

Biomimicryinstitute.org

Clean Clothes Campaign (cleanclothes.org/companies)

Consumer Reports Greener Choices (greenerchoices.org)

Eatwellguide.org

Electronics TakeBack Coalition (electronicstakeback.com)

The EnviroMedia Greenwashing Index (greenwashingindex.com)

Equal Exchange pen pal program (equalexchange.coop/fair-trade-fundraiser-program-pen-pals)

Farmtoschool.org

Foodroutes.org

Good Stuff? A Behind-the-Scenes Guide to the Things We Buy (worldwatch.org/taxonomy/term/44)

Green America National Green Pages (greenpages.org)

Green America Responsible Shopper (responsibleshopper.org)

Greenphone.com

Ibuydifferent.org

Localharvest.org

The Meatrix Trilogy (meatrix.com)

The Otesha Book: From Junk to Funk (http://otesha.ca/files/the_otesha_book.pdf)

The Story of Stuff with Annie Leonard
(storyofstuff.com)

Student Trade Justice Campaign
(tradejusticecampaign.org)

Sustainabletable.org

SweatFree Communities Shop with a Conscience
Consumer Guide (sweatfree.org/shoppingguide)

TakingITGlobal (tigweb.org)

Thinkoutsidethebottle.org

United Students Against Sweatshops
(studentsagainstsweatshops.org)

United Students for Fair Trade (usft.org)

USDA Farmers Market Search
(apps.ams.usda.gov/FarmersMarkets)

Worldchanging.com

Sources

Books

Animal, Vegetable, Miracle: A Year of Food Life
by Barbara Kingsolver (HarperCollins, 2007)

Big Box Reuse by Julia Christensen
(MIT Press, 2008)

*Big-Box Swindle: The True Cost of Mega-Retailers
and the Fight for America's Independent
Businesses* by Stacy Mitchell (Beacon Press, 2006)

*Big Cotton: How a Humble Fiber Created Fortunes,
Wrecked Civilizations, and Put America on the
Map* by Stephen Yafa (Viking, 2005)

Biomimicry: Innovation Inspired by Nature by
Janine M. Benyus (HarperCollins, 1997)

*Born to Buy: The Commercialized Kid and the New
Consumer Culture* by Juliet Schor (Scribner, 2004)

*Bottlemania: How Water Went on Sale and
Why We Bought It* by Elizabeth Royte
(Bloomsbury USA, 2008)

Branded: The Buying and Selling of Teenagers
by Alissa Quart (Basic Books, 2003)

*Buying In: The Secret Dialogue Between What
We Buy and Who We Are* by Rob Walker
(Random House, 2008)

*Cheap: The Real Cost of the Global Trend for
Bargains, Discounts and Consumer Choice* by
David Bosshart (Kogan Page, 2006)

Consuming Kids: The Hostile Takeover of Childhood
by Susan E. Linn (New Press, 2004)

*The Corporation: The Pathological Pursuit of Profit
and Power* by Joel Bakan (Free Press, 2004)

*Cradle to Cradle: Remaking the Way We Make
Things* by William McDonough and Michael
Braungart (North Point Press, 2002)

*Creating a World Without Poverty: Social Business
and the Future of Capitalism* by Muhammad
Yunus (PublicAffairs, 2007)

Crunch: Why Do I Feel So Squeezed? (And Other Unsolved Economic Mysteries) by Jared Bernstein (Berrett-Koehler, 2008)

Deep Economy: The Wealth of Communities and the Durable Future by Bill McKibben (Times Books, 2007)

The Ecology of Commerce: A Declaration of Sustainability by Paul Hawken (HarperCollins, 1993)

ecoDesign: The Sourcebook by Alastair Fuad-Luke (Chronicle Books, 2006)

Fair Trade: A Beginner's Guide by Jacqueline DeCarlo (Oneworld Publications, 2007)

Fast Food Nation: The Dark Side of the All-American Meal by Eric Schlosser (Houghton Mifflin, 2001)

Garbage Land: On the Secret Trail of Trash by Elizabeth Royte (Little, Brown and Company, 2005)

The Gecko's Foot: Bio-inspiration: Engineering New Materials from Nature by Peter Forbes (W. W. Norton & Company, Inc., 2005)

Gone Tomorrow: The Hidden Life of Garbage by Heather Rogers (New Press, 2005)

Green, Inc.: An Environmental Insider Reveals How a Good Cause Has Gone Bad by Christine MacDonald (Lyons Press, 2008)

The Green-Collar Economy: How One Solution Can Fix Our Two Biggest Problems by Van Jones (HarperCollins, 2008)

High Tech Trash: Digital Devices, Hidden Toxics, and Human Health by Elizabeth Grossman (Island Press, 2006)

Holy Cows and Hog Heaven: The Food Buyer's Guide to Farm Friendly Food by Joel Salatin (Polyface Inc., 2004)

Hope's Edge: The Next Diet for a Small Planet by Frances Moore Lappé and Anna Lappé (Putnam, 2002)

Made to Break: Technology and Obsolescence in America by Giles Slade (Harvard University Press, 2006)

Making Globalization Work by Joseph E. Stiglitz (W. W. Norton & Company, Inc., 2006)

No Logo: Taking Aim at the Brand Bullies by Naomi Klein (Picador, 1999)

Not Buying It: My Year without Shopping by Judith Levine (Free Press, 2006)

OBD: Obsessive Branding Disorder by Lucas Conley (PublicAffairs, 2008)

The Omnivore's Dilemma: A Natural History of Four Meals by Michael Pollan (Penguin, 2006)

The Revolution Will Not Be Microwaved: Inside America's Underground Food Movements by Sandor Ellix Katz (Chelsea Green, 2006)

The Rough Guide to Shopping with a Conscience by Duncan Clark and Richie Unterberger (Rough Guides, 2007)

Stuff: The Secret Lives of Everyday Things by John C. Ryan and Alan Thein Durning (Northwest Environment Watch, 1997)

Supercapitalism: The Transformation of Business, Democracy, and Everyday Life by Robert B. Reich (Knopf, 2007)

The Total Beauty of Sustainable Products by Edwin Datschefski (Rotovision, 2001)

The Travels of a T-Shirt in the Global Economy: An Economist Examines the Markets, Power, and Politics of World Trade by Pietra Rivoli (John Wiley & Sons, 2005)

The Wal-Mart Effect: How the World's Most Powerful Company Really Works—and How It's Transforming the American Economy by Charles Fishman (Penguin, 2006)

The Water Business: Corporations versus People by Ann-Christin Sjölander Holland (Zed Books, 2005)

Whose Water Is It? The Unquenchable Thirst of a Water-Hungry World by Bernadette McDonald and Douglas Jehl, eds. (National Geographic, 2003)

Worldchanging: A User's Guide for the 21st Century edited by Alex Steffen (Abrams, 2006)

Articles, Pamphlets, and Reports

"The Afterlife of Cellphones" by Jon Mooallem (*The New York Times*, January 13, 2008)

"At Play on a Field of Trash" by Jessica Snyder Sachs (*Discover* Magazine, June 1997)

"Bad to the Last Drop" by Tom Standage (*The New York Times*, August 1, 2005)

"Behind the Ever-Expanding American Dream House" by Margot Adler (NPR, *All Things Considered*, July 4, 2006)

"Bottled Water Has Contaminants, Too, Study Finds" by Jeff Donn (Associated Press, October 15, 2008)

"CAFOs Uncovered: The Untold Cost of Confined Animal Feeding Operations" by Doug Gurian-Sherman (Union of Concerned Scientists, April 2008)

"Can We Afford to Eat Ethically?" by Siobhan Phillips (Salon.com, April 25, 2009)

"Canadian Teen Discovers Plastic-Bag-Devouring Microbe" by Eoin O'Carroll (*Christian Science Monitor*, May 23, 2008)

"Cell Phones Getting Greener" by Stephen Leahy (Inter Press Service News Agency, January 13, 2007)

"Chemical Used on Crops Could Make You Fat" by Sherry Baker (Naturalnews.com, December 8, 2008)

"Chicken with Arsenic? Is that O.K.?" by Marian Burros (*The New York Times*, April 5, 2006)

"Child Labor Is Back: Children Are Again Sewing Clothing for Major U.S. Companies" (National Labor Committee, 2006)

"The Children Behind Our Cotton" (Environmental Justice Foundation, 2007)

"China Sacks Plastic Bags" by David Biello (*Scientific American*, May 23, 2008)

"Cleaner, Greener Cotton: Impacts and Better Management Practices" (World Wildlife Fund, 2007)

"The Conscious Consumer: Promoting Economic Justice through Fair Trade" by Rose Benz Ericson (Fair Trade Resource Network, 2006)

"The Coolest Little Start-Up in America" by Bo Burlingham (*Inc.*, July 2006)

"The Coolhunt" by Malcolm Gladwell (*The New Yorker*, March 17, 1997)

"Cultivating Poverty: The Impact of US Cotton Subsidies on Africa" (Oxfam, 2002)

"Cutting out the Middlemen, Shoppers Buy Slices of Farms" by Susan Saulny (*The New York Times*, July 10, 2008)

"A 'Dead Zone' in the Gulf of Mexico: Scientists Say Area That Cannot Support Some Marine Life Is Near Record Size" by Joel Achenbach (*The Washington Post*, July 31, 2008)

"The Deadly Chemicals in Cotton" (Environmental Justice Foundation and Pesticide Action Network UK, 2007)

"Dirty Metals: Mining, Communities, and the Environment" (Earthworks and Oxfam America, 2004)

"Down and Dirty: How Carbon Farming, the Practise of Putting CO_2 Back Into the Soil, Can Help Fight Global Warming" by Jay Walljasper (*Ode* magazine, June 2008)

"E-Waste: The Exploding Global Electronic Waste Crisis" (Electronics TakeBack Coalition, 2008)

"Environmental Cost of Shipping Groceries around the World" by Elisabeth Rosenthal (*The New York Times*, April 26, 2008)

"Exporting Harm: The High-Tech Trashing of Asia" (The Basel Action Network and the Silicon Valley Toxics Coalition, 2002)

"Extreme Oil: The Science" (Educational Broadcasting Corporation, 2004 at www.pbs.org)

"Farmer in Chief" by Michael Pollan (*The New York Times*, October 12, 2008)

"Guide to Ending Sweatshops" (Co-op America, 2008)

"Guide to Fair Trade" (Co-op America, 2008)

"Hear Voices? It May Be an Ad" by Andrew Hampp (*Advertising Age*, December 10, 2007)

"High-Tech Trash: Will Your Discarded TV End Up in a Ditch in Ghana?" by Chris Carroll (*National Geographic*, January 2008)

"Hype vs. Hope: Is Corporate Do-Goodery for Real?" by Bill McKibben (*Mother Jones*, November 2006)

"India Reclaims Right to Water from Coca-Cola" by Rev. Thomas John (Presbyterian Hunger Program, *PHP Post*, spring 2009)

"Iowa Farmers Look to Trap Carbon in Soil" by Dan Charles (NPR, *Weekend Edition*, July 15, 2007)

"Is Bottled Water Better?" (Union of Concerned Scientists, June 2007)

"Is Recycling Worth It?" by Alex Hutchison (*Popular Mechanics*, December 2008)

"Lead Toxins Take a Global Round Trip" by Gordon Fairclough (*The Wall Street Journal*, July 12, 2007)

"Livestock's Long Shadow: Environmental Issues and Options" (Food and Agricultural Organization of the United Nations, 2007)

"Localwashing: How Corporate America Is Co-opting 'Local'" by Stacy Mitchell (*Utne Reader*, November–December 2009)

"Message in a Bottle" by Charles Fishman (*Fast Company*, July 2007)

"No Teenage E-Wasteland" by Jay Walljasper (*Ode*, April 2008)

"Not the Same Old Drive-Thru" by Mary Desmond Pinkowish (*Ode*, April 2008)

"Organic Farming 'Could Feed Africa': Traditional Practices Increase Yield by 128 Per Cent in East Africa, Says UN" by Daniel Howden (*The Independent* [UK], October 22, 2008)

"Organic Farming Yields as Good or Better: Study" (Reuters, July 10, 2007)

"Peanut Case Shows Holes in Safety Net" by Michael Moss (*The New York Times*, February 8, 2009)

"Peanut Processor Knowingly Sold Tainted Products" by Lyndsey Layton (*The Washington Post*, January 28, 2009)

"Plants' Rights" by Clay Risen (*The New York Times*, December 12, 2008)

"Plastic-Bag Bans Gaining Momentum around the World" by John Roach (*National Geographic News*, April 4, 2008)

"Product Placement on Reality TV Seems Somehow More Realistic" by Stuart Elliott (*The New York Times*, January 23, 2008)

"Recycling: The Big Picture" by Tom Zeller, Jr. (*National Geographic*, January 2008)

"Rigged Rules and Double Standards: Trade, Globalisation, and the Fight against Poverty" (Oxfam, 2002)

"Science Confirms: You Really Can't Buy Happiness" by Shankar Vedantam (*The Washington Post*, July 3, 2006)

"Self-Storage Nation: Americans Are Storing More Stuff than Ever" by Tom Vanderbilt (*Slate* magazine, July 18, 2005)

"The 'Six Sins of Greenwashing': A Study of Environmental Claims in North American Consumer Markets" (TerraChoice Environmental Marketing Inc., November 2007)

"Supermarkets Take Cut of Fairtrade Cash for Poor Farmers" by Robert Winnett (*The Times* [UK], June 29, 2003)

"The SUV in the Pantry" by Thomas Starrs (*Solar Today*, July/August 2005)

"Tapping Power from Trash" by John Rather (*The New York Times*, September 13, 2008)

"Teenagers' Suit Says McDonald's Made Them Obese" by Marc Santora (*The New York Times*, November 21, 2002)

"Teens Launch 'Girlcott' Against Abercrombie" by Sarah Karnasiewicz (Salon.com, November 3, 2005)

"This Is Your Brain on Advertising" by Amber Haq (*Business Week*, October 8, 2007)

"Toxic Inaction: Why Poisonous, Unregulated Chemicals End Up in Our Blood" by Mark Schapiro (*Harper's Magazine*, October 2007)

"A Turn for the Better: New Technology and Innovative Thinking Are Spinning Old Tires into New Products" by Ursula Sautter (*Ode*, May 2008)

"Vermont Becomes 7th State to Go 'Sweat-Free'" by Chris Garofalo (*The Brattleboro Reformer*, April 29, 2008)

"The Wages of Synergy" by Janine Jaquet (*The Nation*, January 7, 2002)

"Waste Couture: Environmental Impact of the Clothing Industry" (*Environmental Health Perspectives*, September 2007)

"When 'Local' Makes it Big" by Kim Severson (*The New York Times*, May 12, 2009)

Video

Black Gold directed by Marc Francis and Nick Francis (2006)

China Blue directed by Micha X. Peled (2006)

The Corporation directed by Mark Achbar and Jennifer Abbott (2004)

Flow: For Love of Water directed by Irena Salina (2008)

Food, Inc. directed by Robert Kenner (2008)

Frankensteer directed by Marrin Canell and Ted Remerowski (2005)

Fresh directed by Ana Sofia Joanes (2009)

Frontline: Is Wal-Mart Good for America? directed by Rick Young (PBS, 2005)

Frontline: The Merchants of Cool directed by Barak Goodman (PBS, 2001)

Frontline: The Persuaders directed by Rachel Dretzin and Barak Goodman (PBS, 2004)

The Future of Food directed by Deborah Koons Garcia (2004)

An Inconvenient Truth directed by Davis Guggenheim (2006)

King Corn directed by Aaron Woolf (2007)

Life and Debt directed by Stephanie Black (2001)

Maquilapolis directed by Vicky Funari and Sergio de la Torre (2006)

Maxed Out: Hard Times, Easy Credit and the Era of Predatory Lenders directed by James D. Scurlock (2006)

McLibel: The Story of Two People Who Wouldn't Say McSorry directed by Franny Armstrong (2005)

The Meaning of Food directed by Sue McLaughlin (2004)

The Next Industrial Revolution: William McDonough, Michael Braungart and the Birth of the Sustainable Economy directed by Chris Bedford and Shelley Morhaim (2001)

60 Minutes: The Electronic Wasteland produced by Solly Granatstein (CBS News, November 10, 2008)

Super Size Me directed by Morgan Spurlock (2004)

Wal-Mart: The High Cost of Low Price directed by Robert Greenwald (2005)

What Would Jesus Buy? directed by Rob VanAlkemade (2007)

Groups and Web Sites

Adbusters
adbusters.org

Behind the Label
behindthelabel.org

Big Box Tool Kit
bigboxtoolkit.com

Campaign for a Commercial-Free Childhood
commercialexploitation.org

The Campaign to Label Genetically Engineered Foods
thecampaign.org

Center for Food Safety
centerforfoodsafety.org

Clean Clothes Campaign (United Kingdom)
cleanclothes.org

Commercial Alert
commercialalert.org

Conscious Consumer (Center for a
    New American Dream)
newdream.org

Corporate Accountability International
stopcorporateabuse.org

Electronics TakeBack Coalition
electronicstakeback.com

Environmental Justice Foundation
ejfoundation.org

Fair Trade Federation
fairtradefederation.org

Fair Trade Resource Network
fairtraderesource.org

Farm to School
farmtoschool.org

Global Exchange
globalexchange.org

Global Youth Action Network
youthlink.org

Grassroots Recycling Network
grrn.org

Green America Responsible Shopper
responsibleshopper.org

Consumer Reports Greener Choices
greenerchoices.org

Institute for Local Self-Reliance
ilsr.org

Media Awareness Network
media-awareness.ca

The National Labor Committee
nlcnet.org

Natural Resources Defense Council
nrdc.org

The New Rules Project
newrules.org

Oxfam International
oxfam.org/en/campaigns/trade

The Story of Stuff with Annie Leonard
storyofstuff.com

Sustainable Table
sustainabletable.org

Sweatfree Communities Shop with a
    Conscience Consumer Guide
sweatfree.org/shoppingguide

Union of Concerned Scientists
ucsusa.org

United Students Against Sweatshops
studentsagainstsweatshops.org

United Students for Fair Trade
usft.org

Worldchanging
worldchanging.com

Worldwatch Institute
worldwatch.org

Index